The World of
Guitars

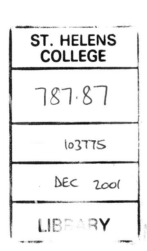
This edition was published in 1999
by Greenwich Editions
10 Blenheim Court
Brewery Road
London, N7 9NT
© Copyright, Paris, 1997

ISBN: 0 86288 282 6
Printed in Spain

The World of
Guitars

CHRISTIAN SEGURET

Photographs by
Matthieu Prier

GREENWICH EDITIONS

The history of the guitar is a bit like the history of mankind—very few instruments have been so closely synchronized with every step of the human experience. To discover the guitar's origins, trace its evolution, and revisit its epic adventures, one has only to read between the lines of history books.

The result of a lengthy evolution, the guitar eventually found its place in the court of Louis XIV, as well as in Venetian palaces. Yet it was also at home in the modest dwellings of Parisian street urchins and Catalan laborers. While the traditional violin remained steadfastly true to the canons determined by a genius luthier, the more progressive guitar defied all rules and regulations, blossoming in every latitude and under the most unexpected guises. It was constantly modified, by both expert luthiers and self-taught crafts- men, who often initiated some of its most significant muta- tions. The guitar was as com- fortable in the hands of a vir- tuoso as in the hands of a dab- bling amateur.

Some guitars are swapped in schoolyard corners; others are purchased for astronomical prices in the most prestigious auction houses. The guitar is the most democratic of high- society instruments, an aristo- crat befriended by the Reds, a princess who flirts with scoun- drels. The guitar belongs in glittering Italian theaters as well as in smoky Mississippi honky-tonks. It was revered by hippies in the sixties, yet re- mains the object of desire for contemporary creators. This is an instrument that embodies the art of eternal metamorphosis.

Every migration, artistic revo- lution, and major discovery in human history has left its mark on the role and design of the guitar. Even its shape has

changed with the ebb and flow of human tastes. When conquistadors set out to conquer the New World, they brought with them the guitar's ancestor, the *vihuela*—unusual descendants of this stringed instrument can still be found in South America today, all of them a result of an evolution that was parallel, but totally independent, to that of the guitar. As envisioned by the Voboams, the guitar was as round and embellished as a Watteau belle, yet it also managed to conform to the ethics of Quaker simplicity in Christian Friedrich Martin's adopted America. In seventeenth-century Vienna, it was practically crushed under the weight of sculpted ivory cherubs. Under the Andalusian sun, it was austere, suffering, and proud, much like the dancers it accompanied. And at the turn of the century, when a new artistic style was making Paris metro stations blossom, the guitar featured scrolls, carvings, and inlays that might have been signed by Mucha.

The history of the guitar is also distinguished by technical innovations and unfortunate disappearances: when ivory, tortoise shell, and rare varieties of wood became scarce, synthetic ersatz, chrome, and graphite quickly replaced them, creating an ever-changing, modern look. Although purists have sometimes denounced the instrument's swift adoption of the latest materials, the guitar's longevity is due in part to this very adaptability—and also to its accessibility to the general public.

As long as school children save their pennies to buy their first one, and as long as talented musicians continue to be inspired by them, the guitar will remain the universal instrument we know today.

For all these reasons, and more, its story deserves telling.

~ Contents ~

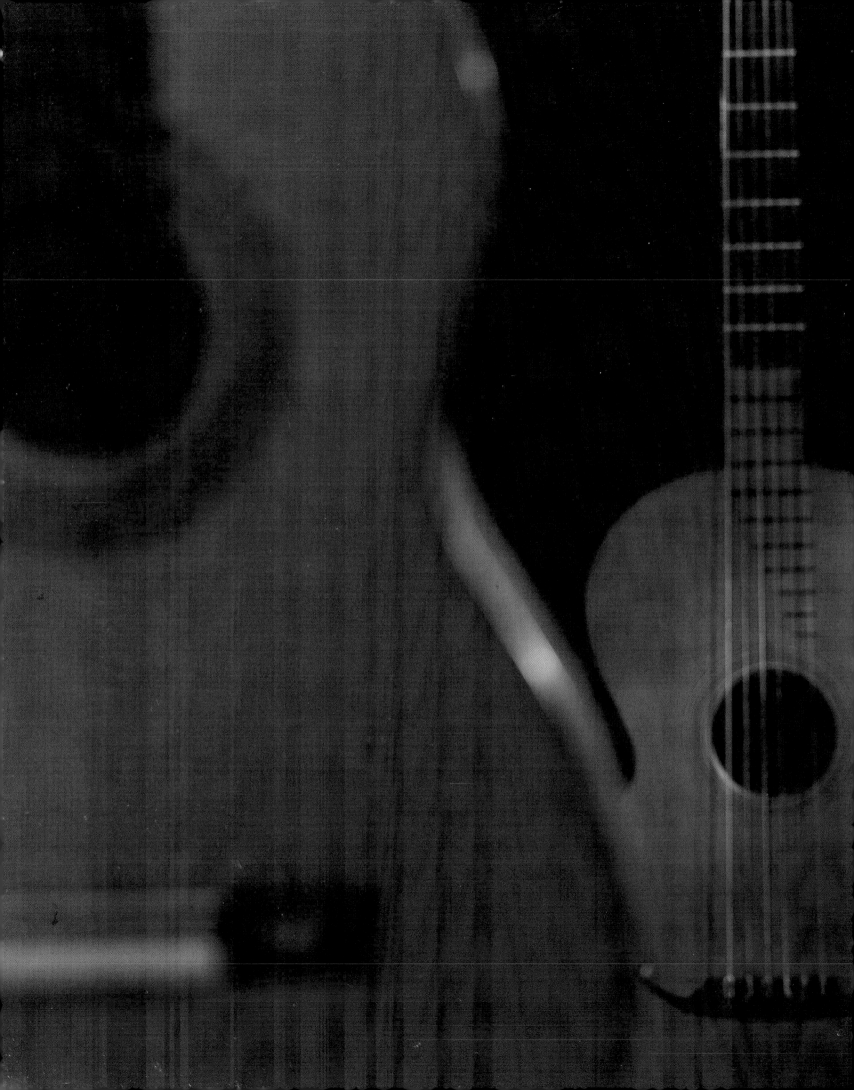

From the Baroque ~ to the ~ Modern Classical Guitar

From its first mention in thirteenth-century literature to the contemporary model established by Antonio de Torres in the mid-nineteenth century, the guitar has survived a chaotic evolution of complex twists and turns. Thirteenth-century Spanish illustrations have been discovered that depict musicians holding *guitarras latinas*, which look remarkably like smaller-sized contemporary guitars. Since no actual guitars survive from this period, however, it is difficult to definitively distinguish these instruments from their cousins: the lutes, mandores, and mandolins.

Spain is truly the birthplace of the guitar. Early forms of the Spanish instrument came in two versions: the vihuela and the guitar. The former, more aristocratic and elaborately constructed, generally possessed six, or sometimes seven, sets of double strings. The guitar, considered a "poor relation" of the vihuela, had only four sets of strings. These groupings of two (or three) strings, tuned in octaves or in unison, were called "courses." The standard number of courses varied over the years and differed also from region to region. For example, five courses were typical in the seventeenth century, while later on, the number grew to six. The first known guitar with six single strings was built in 1773 by the French luthier François Lupot, in Orléans.

Over time, these instruments evolved: the curves rounded out, the waists narrowed, and the rims, or sides, became perpendicular to the top. These features eventually differentiated the guitar from other stringed instruments of the same family, such as the lute and mandolin.

From the Torres (1884) (in the foreground) to the Pacherel (1834) and the Tesler (1618), two and a half centuries of guitar history are united at the Museum of the City of Nice.

The Genesis of the Guitar

The first hero in the history of guitars may well be the man who, a few millennia ago, decided to tie a string to a bow, make it vibrate, and amplify the sound by attaching a gourd to it. From this seed of an idea grew a whole group of instruments whose general principle was to produce sound by way of a vibrating string. From these forerunners developed the kithara, a Greek lyre that was adopted by the Romans, and from whose name the word "guitar" originates. During the eighth century, Arab invaders introduced into Europe instruments such as the oud and the rebab, which in turn inspired the evolution of the lute. During the Renaissance, however, the guitar began to emerge as somthing distinct from these instruments, as well as from the mandolin and, in general, all other oval-shaped instruments with rounded backs—the guitar's distinguishing features being a narrower waist and a form with more curves.

The oldest surviving guitars, dating from the late sixteenth century, had much smaller bodies and broader waists than modern instruments. They also sometimes had rounded backs—made of adjoining strips of wood, like the body of a boat—that were, nevertheless, attached to the soundboard by perpendicular rims, or sides. The scale length (that is, the total length of the vibrating strings between the bridge and the nut) was considerably shorter than that of a modern model, and these early instruments generally had five courses of strings. Despite these differences, these instruments looked more or less like the guitars of today. The five-course guitar most likely originated in Spain, and from the sixteenth century onward, its popularity grew across various European countries such as France and Italy. Most surviving guitars from this period are Italian, but it would be incorrect to conclude that the Italians were the predominant guitar makers of the era. These surviving instruments were originally built for the prestigious and wealthy elite, their exceptional craftsmanship making them more likely to be cherished, preserved, and collected. Their French, and especially Spanish, counterparts were more popular, played often, and, being well-worn, were less likely to survive the centuries. By that time, the guitar had already gained popularity with the common people; its accessibility encouraged even the simplest folks to learn a few chords and play the *rasgueado*, a basic strum every beginner enjoys learning.

The universal popularity of the guitar enraged musical authorities of the day. One such detractor, Sebastián de Covarrubias Oroco, wrote in 1611: "The guitar is not worth more than a cowbell; it is so easy to play that there is not a single farm boy who is not a guitarist."

Rosettes

The decorative inlay around the soundhole is known as the "rosette." They gave craftsmen a chance to showcase their skills. The center of each soundhole is adorned with a rosette made of decoupage parchment adhered in several layers, creating a relief effect. The rosettes are further embellished with borders inlayed with mother-of-pearl, ivory or ebony. (From top to bottom: **René Voboam, Jean Christophle, Giovanni Tesler**).

Jean-Joseph Fontanelli's Bass Lute (1773)

Despite its similar appearance, the lute is actually an instrument completely distinct from the guitar, and evolved in an entirely different way. The mandolin, which appeared at many stages in the guitar's history, shares more similarities with the lute. Both instruments feature an oval-shaped body without a waist, and a vaulted back made of adjoining strips of wood. The rosette of this superb lute, unlike those of the guitars at left, is carved directly into the spruce of the soundboard. The elaborate intricacy of the ivory inlays on the fingerboard is a testament to the talent of Fontanelli, the Bologna-based craftsman who created some of the most beautiful pieces of his era.

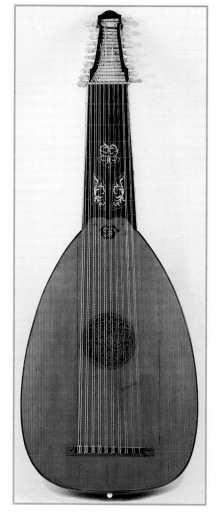

The Baroque Guitar

The design and level of ornamentation on seventeenth-century instruments differed considerably from one country to another, but all schools of guitar making shared a few common principles. Very fine spruce was normally used to construct the soundboard, which often extended onto the fingerboard. The fingerboard featured gut frets which were attached around the neck—their haphazard placement often affected the tuning. The bridge, which was not moved back to a center position until the mid-eighteenth century, was at this time placed far from the soundhole, near the base of the guitar.

Despite these common attributes, important regional variations did exist. Instruments built in Spain were of very simple craftsmanship. Similarly, those made in Cremona by Antonio Stradivarius, rarely remembered for his guitars, were as austere as the violins that made him famous.

On the other hand, German-made instruments, like the ones by Joachim Tielke, were highly adorned, often with ebony and ivory inlay. Guitars built in northern Italy in the early seventeenth century were also extremely ornate. The Italians tastefully combined mother-of-pearl, ebony, and ivory to create instruments that still survive today as visual delights, though they can no longer be played. Such is the fate of the existing instruments made by Giovanni Tesler in Ancona.

Today, only two instruments attributed to this major luthier are in existence: the guitar in the Museum of the City of Nice is the only one to have been officially authenticated; the other, in the Royal College of Music in London, has been attributed to Tesler mainly because of the initials "G. T." on the top of the soundboard.

The Tesler guitar shown on this page is typical of seventeenth-century Italian lutherie. Its inlayed herringbone motif can be found on other guitars of the period, such as that made by Matteo Sellas, one in a long family line of Venetian luthiers. The Sellas guitar is housed in the Victoria and Albert Museum in London. It is interesting to note that both Sellas and Tesler were actually Tyrolese craftsmen who settled in Italy. Many such Germanic luthiers migrated to northern Italy in the early seventeenth century, and they had a significant influence on instrument making in the area.

It follows, then, that the history of the guitar is one made up of an eclectic blend of ideas and techniques.

Giovanni Tesler Guitar (1618)

This guitar, in beautiful condition, is one of the very few that has survived intact from this era. The table is embellished with black putty motifs, while the fingerboard is decorated with mother-of-pearl rectangles and bordered with ivory. The back and rim of this instrument are decorated with a herringbone inlay made up of alternating light and dark wood. The fine workmanship of this instrument suggests that it was made for someone of importance.

Giovanni Tesler Guitar

This guitar, made by Giovanni Tesler in Ancona in 1618, is typical of seventeenth-century Italian lutherie.
The ebony bridge was intended to hold five double courses of strings; however, the headstock is fitted with only nine pegs. This discrepancy would suggest that this instrument, like most of the era, was modified over time, and is no longer in its original condition.

The French School

Luthiers of Louis XIV's Court

The French school of guitar making began under the reign of Louis XIV. The guitars produced at that time were less ornate than the ones made by the Italians and were adorned with more geometrical motifs. Furthermore, they featured flat backs. The most famous members of this school were the Voboams, a family of luthiers that dominated the seventeenth century. René, the first of the line, was followed by Alexandre, and then by his son Jean. Their instruments possessed similar characteristics, which were often adopted by other French luthiers of the day. The Voboams were particularly fond of using a diagonal border motif around the soundboard. This decoration was found on most French instruments of the time, as can be seen in many engravings from that period, especially in drawings and paintings by Jean Antoine Watteau, for whom the guitar was a favorite subject. Jean and René Voboam also made extensive use of tortoise shell, which they regularly applied to the backs and rims of their instruments. This material, like ivory, would later become increasingly scarce and would eventually be replaced by synthetic materials starting in the early twentieth century.

It was also the Voboams who can be credited for the disappearance of decorative inlay from the center of guitar soundboards. This ornamentation, often spectacular from an aesthetic point of view, unfortunately tended to undermine the acoustics of the instrument.

Guitar attribued to René Voboam (17th century)

This instrument is believed to have been built by the famous Parisian luthier René Voboam. It features all the characteristic qualities of this favorite craftsman of Louis XIV's court. Of particular interest are the superb tortoise-shell marquetry on the back and rims, and the diagonal inlays of alternating ebony and ivory, dubbed pistagne, around the table and down the center of the back. The fingerboard is also adorned with an intricate floral ivory motif, inlaid in ebony. Unfortunately, this instrument has been restored several times, and the soundboard was replaced during the last century.

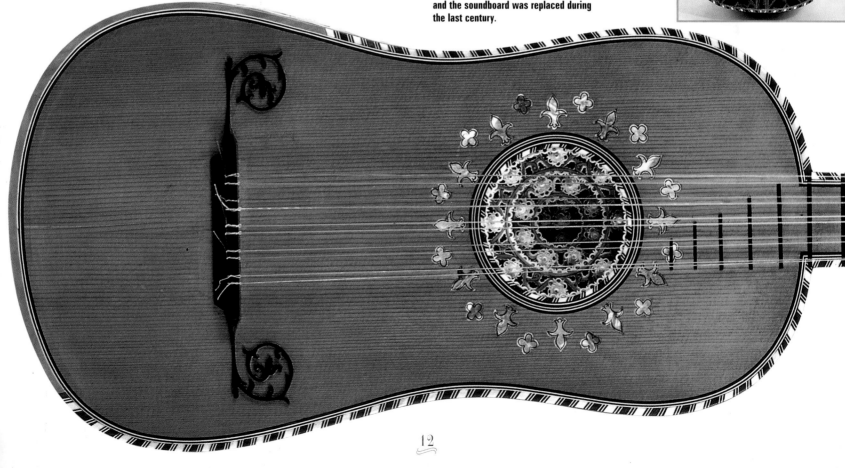

Jean Christophle "Coffin" Case (1645)

Guitar makers of this period often crafted their own cases, sometimes out of expensive woods such as mahogany or rosewood—woods more commonly used today to build the guitars themselves! The evocative shape of this case, known today as the "coffin shape," found its way across the Atlantic and was used by C.F. Martin and other early American builders.

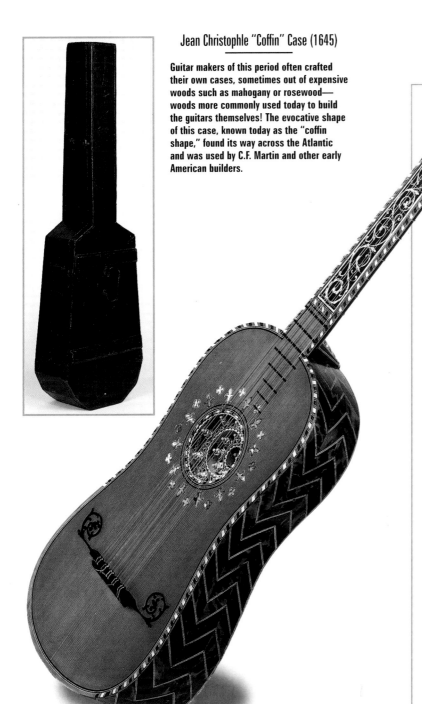

Guitar Restoration

The restoration of historical instruments is an exciting and complex profession. Guitars restored and kept in museums actually have two functions. First, they allow us to admire and enjoy their superb aesthetic qualities, and they inspire us to imagine the generations of musicians who might have played upon them. These guitars, however, also provide researchers and luthiers, present and future, with a gold mine of information about construction methods of the past. It is therefore extremely important to protect them from the adverse effects of time, while at the same time avoiding, as much as possible, any alteration to their original characteristics. This double mission serves as a guideline to all guitar restorers. They must respect and understand the craftsman's techniques of yesteryear: construction principles, which were patterned after the technical knowledge and musical rules of the day; glues which were, of course, different; and also materials, such as ivory or tortoise shell, which have become scarce and are now rarely used. In addition to all these technical qualifications, an expert restorer must also possess a good historical background in order to evaluate the date of construction of a given instrument, spot potential previous restorations, and eventually correct them if they have not been properly executed.

Below, a Voboam guitar is being repaired at the Parisian workshop of Rosyne Charle. This master craftsman, who specializes in repairing and restoring guitars and other stringed instruments, regularly works for the instrument museums of Nice and Paris.

Hybrids

Lyre and Harp Guitars

For almost two centuries, the guitar evolved very little; but eventually, by the late eighteenth century, the guitar began to undergo tremendous changes—one such transformation that occurred at that time was the shift to six single strings. This change evolved gradually, with the instrument first switching from five to six double courses. A good example of this transition is illustrated on the opposite page with a Gérard Deleplanque guitar, built in Lille in 1771.

At the same time, some French luthiers were already experimenting with guitars with six single strings, similar to those we know today. François Lupot of Orléans was one such experimental guitar maker. In fact, an instrument built by him in 1773 is the oldest six-string guitar in existence today. In the 1780s, this new six-string trend caught on throughout all of Europe—with the notable exception of Spain. It was also around this time that some unusual instruments started appearing in France: hybrids between the guitar and the lyre of antiquity.

These *lyres-guitares*, as they were known in France, first appeared in response to the resurgence of interest in the

classics and antiquities that had gripped Europe at that time. Playing these instruments, the intellectuals of the time could imagine themselves transported back into history, to a place under the grand columns of the Parthenon. Madame de Staël, for instance, was often seen with a lyre-guitar in her hands. She was in turn emulated by many high-society women who commissioned increasingly ornate instruments from the busy, overjoyed luthiers. Eventually, the piano-forte, together with the advent of the romantic movement, forced these odd instruments into retirement in the attics of many aristocratic homes.

A lyre-guitar was tuned like a guitar, and the player was supposed to hold and play it like one. This was not an easy task considering its size and weight. Nonetheless, they were sometimes used in concert by musicians like Giuliani. Another oddity, albeit a less cumbersome one, made its appearance in France at about the same time: the arpiguitare, a sort of harp soundbox above which was fixed a guitar fingerboard. The French luthier Pacquet from Marseilles specialized in the construction of this unusual instrument.

The Lyre-guitar (18th century)

This hybrid instrument was fairly commonplace in the eighteenth century. Despite its silhouette, reminiscent of an antique harp, it was held and played like a guitar. With its peghead ornamented in golden acanthus leaves, and its finely carved sides, the craftsmanship in this type of instrument owes as much to traditional furniture-making techniques as it does to classic lutherie. This particular instrument, though unsigned, looks very much like a guitar preserved at Yale University, which is signed by a "Charles," based in Marseilles. The guitar's label identifies him as: "Master luthier from Paris, nephew of Sieur Guersan." In fact, this same "Guersan" happens to be one of the most famous Parisian luthiers of the eighteenth century.

Pacquet's Harp-guitar (1785)

This instrument is typical of the work of certain French luthiers of this era; Paquet of Marseilles, in particular, specialized in this type of hybrid construction. In some ways, this instrument, with its elongated soundbox, is reminiscent of a harp. Also harp-like is the angle of the strings relative to the soundboard. On the other hand, the neck, frets, and tuning would all classify this instrument in the guitar family.

François Breton's Lyre-guitar (ca. 1800)

François Breton was a craftsman from Mirecourt, one of the capitals of European instrument making. This little town, nestled the Vosges mountains, is home to one of the world's oldest lutherie schools, where generations of skilled artisans have honed their craft. This lyre-guitar, of a more modest design than the previous one, features an interesting solid ebony neck topped with an unusual, circular-shaped peghead. Two brass bars reinforce the instrument.

Pacquet's Peghead

This harp-guitar peghead is reminiscent of the sculpted versions found on certain cellos or double-basses, with its seven ebony pegs fitted to the side and activated by simple friction. The beautiful motifs of pearls and acanthus leaves, as well as the gargoyle head that crowns the instrument, exemplify perfect mastery in wood carving. Note also the original brass "capodastre." This accessory, still in use today, is used to reduce the scale of the instrument and therefore change keys (for instance, to accompany a vocalist), without changing already mastered fingerings.

Gérard Deleplanque Guitar (1771)

With its six courses, this guitar is a good example of the transition toward the romantic model with six individual strings. Note that the frets are no longer made of gut as on seventeenth-century instruments, nor has Deleplanque as yet adopted the metal frets generally used after the late eighteenth century. Instead, the frets of this guitar are made of bone (on the ebony fingerboard), or of ebony (for the last two frets on the table).

The Romantic Guitar

The Advent of the Contemporary Guitar

At the beginning of the nineteenth century, the guitar evolved into the "romantic" model. Larger, plainer, and with a narrower waist, its overall shape was relatively similar to that of today's guitars. The instruments illustrated on these pages, made in Nice by François Bastien and Pierre Pacherel, are typical examples of these first romantic instruments.

A number of innovations altered the guitar and gave it a new and attractive personality. It was about that time, for example, that the strings, instead of being simply attached by knots (as they still are on classical guitars), began to be attached to the bridge by way of wooden pegs. Later, this system of anchoring the strings would be found on American-made instruments. Beginning in the 1820s, the guitar's fingerboard extended onto the soundboard, often as far as the soundhole. It was around this same period that the German luthier Johann Stauffer introduced an experimental fingerboard that was elevated over the top of the soundboard, leaving the latter free to vibrate. This innovation was ignored by most of his colleagues for a long time, but was reintroduced on an industrial level in the 1920s by Gibson's engineers in America. Ironically, Gibson's main competitor at that time was the Martin Company, whose founder, Christian Friedrich Martin, apprenticed with none other than Stauffer!

In the early nineteenth century, luthiers continued to experiment with the number of strings on the guitar. Since the six-string model was a fairly recent innovation, adventurous luthiers felt free to drift away from this standard, sometimes adding an extra treble or bass string to their instruments. Such was the case of René Lacôte, the most popular Parisian luthier of the first half of the nineteenth century, who built seven-string guitars for Napoléon Coste, a pupil of Fernando Sor. At least two such guitars still exist, and there is every reason to believe that

Napoléon Coste

Guitarist Napoléon Coste presents a collection of remarkable guitars, some with extra bass strings and extended scale lengths.

Lacôte built more. These instruments featured an additional bass string, tuned to D, as well as unique accessories, such as a finger-rest or a tailpiece adorned with a Maltese cross. These seven-string instruments were also used by the Russian classical virtuoso Andreas Ossipovitch Sichra, and later, by such jazz guitarists as Bucky Pizarelli. Lacôte also came up with a system that allowed the player to lock the string on the pegs once they were tuned. A similar system later reappeared in the 1980s.

Lacôte, ever the innovator, can also be credited with the first scalloped fingerboard. On this type of fingerboard, the fingertips of the left hand, which are positioned between two frets to play a given note, do not directly touch the fingerboard surface. The fingertips are thus provided an unusual freedom of movement, allowing them to achieve wider glissandos and vibratos. On the other hand, the intonation is less reliable. An identical system reappeared in the 1980s, when rock guitarist Yngwie Malmsteem repopularized it.

Bridges and mustaches

The bridge, which for a long time had been adorned with an intricate "mustache" motif, gradually acquired a less ornate profile during the nineteenth century. At the same time, the practice of anchoring strings by a simple knot (center photo), which is still found on classical guitars today, gave way to a system of wooden fasteners or "pins." These tapered bridge pins hold the ends of the strings in place when inserted into holes pierced in the bridge.

Pierre Pacherel Guitar (1834)

This is a good example of a French romantic period guitar. It features a svelte outline, with accentuated curves, and little decoration. Pierre Pacherel, originally from Mirecourt, did his apprenticeship with Jean-Baptiste Vuillaume, one of the greatest luthiers of the early nineteenth century. He later perfected his craft in Genoa and Turin, and finally settled in Nice, where he produced many highly regarded instruments of the time.

René Lacôte Guitar (ca. 1830)

In the guitar world, no one was more popular than René Lacôte in the Paris scene of the early nineteenth century. He produced numerous instruments, all beautifully crafted, and was also responsible for a number of guitar innovations. This particular guitar was probably built for guitarist Napoléon Coste, who is pictured on page 16 with a similar instrument. These seven-string guitars might have been delivered to Coste without their distinctive accessories: the decorated tailpiece and finger-rest. It seems that Coste customized the instruments himself before selling them to his students, a common practice at that time.

François Bastien Guitar (1826)

The guitars of Bastien, a Niçois luthier, were beautifully crafted and elegantly proportioned, but were made with modest materials and featured no superfluous ornamentation. This guitar has a "palette" headstock, whose curves repeat the shape of the larger instrument. Note the unusual oval soundhole; a similar feature appeared on Selmer guitars in the 1930s. The bridge mustache is not original—a faint outline of the original crescent bridge, which was more common at that time, can still be made out on the soundboard.

Antonio de Torres

Father of the Modern Guitar

For many years, Cadiz was the capital of Spanish lutherie, followed closely by Seville and Granada. Luthiers from these three cities soon established a basic guitar of simple elegance, with a slender headstock and pronounced curves. They also adopted a preference for certain woods which were overlooked in other parts of Europe, particularly rosewood and cypress, which is still used today on flamenco guitars. Since the primary function of these instruments was to be played, decoration was kept to a bare minimum. The pragmatic Spanish luthiers understood, long before anyone else, that an overly decorated soundboard was restricting, and that a decorated fingerboard, while beautiful, was uncomfortable for the player. As early as the eighteenth century, the peghead of these guitars had become large, flat, and equipped with simple friction pegs. (Such characteristics are still found on flamenco guitars.) Although the rest of Europe had converted to guitars with six single strings, Spain remained attached to six-course instruments for a long time, perhaps because the superior volume they generated was perfectly suited to their primary role: accompanying song and dance. It was not until about 1820 that the Spanish adopted the six-string guitar; and it was not until the middle of the century, with the innovations of Torres, "the Stradivari of the guitar," that the instrument evolved into the classic form we know today.

Little is known about the early days of Torres. He was born in 1817 near Almería, and according to Emilio Pujol, he probably did his apprenticeship with José Pernas in Granada. He then settled in Seville in the early 1850s and opened a shop on Cerrágería Street. Soon after, guitarists like Julián Arcas, and,

most notably, Francisco Tárrega (1852–1909), became faithful clients and his best ambassadors. Despite this support, his business declined and he was forced into other work from 1869 to 1880. In 1880, he settled in Almería, where he resumed his craft and remained until his death in 1892. According to his biographer, José Romanillos, Torres built approximately 320 guitars during his career, of which only 66 are in existence today.

Antonio de Torres had an important influence on guitar making for many reasons. He enlarged the body of the guitar and accentuated its proportions, while maintaining the narrow waist. He also used lighter materials and thinner soundboards so that, despite their increased size, his instruments were no heavier than earlier models. And, through a process of trial and error, he instituted sizes and proportions for his guitars that were based on geometrical logic. All

Antonio de Torres Guitar (1884)

This remarkable instrument dates from Torres' second period, when he was based in Almería. Its simplicity, combined with its perfect craftsmanship, show that the Spanish master had at that time reached the pinnacle of his art. Guitars made by Torres are extremely rare, and this instrument, conserved at the Museum of Nice, is in excellent condition. The fingerboard and the peghead of the instrument have, however, been altered during several restorations, most recently in 1971.

Torres established most of the standards of modern classical guitar construction. This rosewood bridge, for instance, was modeled after patterns Torres developed and which have been adopted by most of his successors. Notice that the two "wings" of the bridge are identical in length to half of the central bridge where the saddle is located. The label, visible through the strings and the soundhole, reads: "D. Antonio de Torres, Constructor de Guitarras en Sevilla. Vive Hoy en Almeria, Calle Real, N°80." The soundboard is made from two pieces of symmetrically aligned spruce, arranged so that the growth lines increase in width as they reach the outer edges of the guitar.

of these elements can still be found on guitars today. Torres' most significant contribution to lutherie, however, was his bracing system. Much like a race car's engine, an acoustic guitar's braces are invisible to the casual observer but make all the difference in the world. A guitar's bracing system is made up of thin pieces of wood attached to the underside of the soundboard. Their role is to keep the soundboard from collapsing, while allowing it maximum freedom of movement.

For a long time, guitar braces were simple crosses of rather thick wood attached to either side of the soundhole, and they considerably affected the vibrations of the instrument. It was probably in southern Spain, toward the end of the eighteenth century, that the first fan braces, similar to the ones known today, appeared. A guitar built in 1763 by Francisco Pérez of Cadiz was already equipped with fan braces—and they do not seem to be the result of a subsequent restoration. Later on, luthiers from Cadiz (such as Joseph Benedit, and Juan and José Pagés) or from Seville (such as Francisco Sanguino) improved upon the principle of fan bracing, which Torres further perfected when he came upon the scene.

Torres considered the soundboard and the braces of the guitar to be the central force of the instrument. He once demonstrated this theory by building an instrument featuring a spruce table and his now-famous bracing design, to which he attached a cardboard body. According to the few lucky listeners at the time, such as Domingo Prat, this instrument had an outstanding tonal quality. This very instrument can still be admired today at the Instrument Museum of the Barcelona Conservatory; unfortunately, its poor condition makes a repetition of the historic experiment an impossibility.

After years of experimentation, Torres came up with his famous design of seven braces displayed in a fan pattern between the soundhole and the guitar's lower bout. This system remains the one preferred by most contemporary guitar makers, who may sometimes add a few personal adaptations to the basic design. Torres also finally decided upon a standard scale length of 25 1/2 inches for his guitars; he elongated the fingerboard, and he freed his instruments from all superfluous decoration. Thus, the modern classical guitar was born.

Legendary Luthiers

Major Names in Contemporary Guitars

Robert Bouchet

This Parisian luthier was a professional painter and an amateur guitarist. He built his first instrument in 1946, encouraged by his friend Julian Gómez Ramírez (who had done his own apprenticeship under José Ramírez I). Bouchet soon emerged as a first-rate luthier, always guided by a strong aesthetic sense—one that inspired him to go as far as hand-engraving the labels of his instruments. His large, well-balanced guitars have been used by concert musicians such as Alexandre Lagoya and Julian Bream.

Torres never took an apprentice. After his death, Madrid became the capital of classical guitar construction, thanks to a group of young luthiers in the early twentieth century that included Vincente Arias, José Ramírez I, and his brother, Manuel. The Ramírez brothers established a veritable dynasty, with José I passing on his shop to José II, and later onto José III. José Ramírez and Bernabe were among the first to replace spruce, thus far the most commonly used wood in sound-board construction, with cedar. Cedar was more readily available, but some experts questioned its long-term acoustic qualities, doubting that it possessed cedar's ability to improve with age. Ramírez was also one of the first to reinforce the necks of his guitars with a piece of ebony.

Quality classical guitar construction spread rapidly throughout the whole of Spain, and then abroad. For example, Ignacio Fleta in Barcelona, and Antonio Montero in Granada were producing outstanding instruments. Fleta, a pioneer in the field, cautiously ventured away from the bracing concept standardized by Torres, and came up with a number of interesting innovations. For instance, he applied a varnish on the inside of his guitars to improve their reflecting power. And his instruments, which had a fairly large upper bout, began to adopt an outline more and more like that of early nineteenth-century guitars.

In France, Robert Bouchet built only a few dozen guitars over his short career, which did not even begin until he was in his forties. These rare instruments are, understandably, highly prized by collectors today. Originally a painter and guitar aficionado, Bouchet built instruments with exceptional aesthetic qualities and with interesting bracing innovations.

Many important guitar innovations were also initiated by concert guitarists themselves. Faced with the growing dimensions of concert halls and the need for greater volume, these musicians urged some luthiers to increase the scale length of

Manuel Contreras Guitar (1992)

This guitar from the Madrid-based luthier, who passed away in the mid-1990s, is built so that no critical part of the instrument is in direct contact with the musician's body. The sides are therefore doubled at strategic points where the knee or the forearm of the player might inhibit the vibrations. Similarly, the back is outfitted with a double board. This type of instrument is reminiscent of the double-soundboard guitars that emerged throughout the history of European lutherie, particularly in models built by Maccaferri or Gelas.

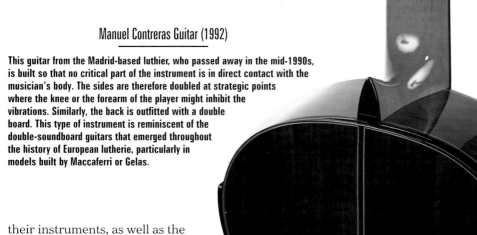

Manuel Contreras Peghead

This beautifully decorated peghead is quite unusual; on the vast majority of classical guitars, ornamentation is kept to a bare minimum.

their instruments, as well as the size of the soundbox. Andrés Segovia was one of the major initiators of these changes. He had Ramírez build him instruments with a scale length of 26 1/4 inches. This substantial increase required the guitarist to stretch his hand much greater distances. Also, as the string was lengthened, more tension was needed to reach the same frequency while tuning the guitar. This additional tension, transmitted by the bridge, meant that the guitar's volume was significantly increased, but also made the musician's task more difficult because of the heightened string resistance and greater finger stretches required.

Segovia, who had extremely flexible hands, was not hindered by these challenges, but average guitarists soon developed problems such as tendinitis from playing instruments ill-suited to their abilities. Ultimately, the overall scale length of guitars increased only by about a half inch in the past century. Considering that our average heights have increased by about six inches over the same period of time, this evolution seems quite reasonable.

All these guitar makers also created handmade instruments, often scrupulously following the specific requests of the musicians themselves. Their guitars obviously had little in common in terms of quality, attention to detail, and value, with today's factory-made instruments. Nowadays we must be aware that a luthier's label adhered to a guitar does not necessarily imply the type of old-fashioned craftsmanship we might imagine. The picture of a solitary luthier, in the calm and comforting disorder of his Gepetto-like workshop, smelling faintly of resin and glue, is not very realistic. When one considers that Bouchet built only 156 guitars in his whole career, while around the world there are more than 25,000 instruments bearing the Ramírez label, one realizes that traditional lutherie ranges from the solitary artisan devoted to his craft to highly trained teams of skilled professionals.

Paulino Bernabe Guitar (far left), Manuel Contreras Guitar (left)

Here are two beautiful examples of the Madrid school of lutherie. The tradition seems destined to survive, as the sons of both these luthiers were educated in the Ramírez workshop and are now ready to carry on where their parents left off. These two instruments feature the woods most commonly used in classical guitar construction: rosewood (Brazilian, for these two guitars) for the body, and spruce for the top. Contreras also constructed many instruments using cedar.

Contemporary Luthiers

A Universal Tradition

Long limited to Spain, the classical guitar began to appear elsewhere throughout the world in the early twentieth century, a trend helped by great Spanish virtuosos such as Andrés Segovia, who was indeed an important ambassador for the instrument. (According to legend, famed luthier Manuel Ramírez gave his first guitar to young Segovia, who at the time was too poor to buy the instrument of his dreams.)

Luthiers soon established themselves in various European countries, and eventually in the United States and Japan. In Germany, for example, Herman Hauser crafted instruments of outstanding quality. He was the first non-Spanish luthier to acquire an international reputation in the field of classical guitars, and his instruments were adopted by such first-rate guitarists as Segovia and Julian Bream. His son followed in his footsteps with similar success. In England, the talented David Rubio also made a name for himself, while in the United States the school of lutherie was led by Manuel Velásquez. Today, many young guitar makers are following the path he paved for them.

Similarly, the Japanese, always adept at duplicating, turned out to be excellent luthiers—the millions of classical guitarists found in Japan today are a testament to their success. Masaru Kohno can probably be considered the father of the Japanese school of lutherie. Kohno crafted quality instruments and inspired some of his younger colleagues, such as Kazuo Sato.

Modern classical guitars have an overall design that is quite similar to the Torres model. Careful inspection, however, will reveal certain aspects—mainly in its internal construction—that distinguish it from the original established by the Spanish master. Manufacturers and acoustic engineers, such as American scientist Michael Kasha, have developed revolutionary concepts that affect guitar braces and bridges, but their ideas have never been very well received by concert players. This might be due to the inability of the musicians to adapt to these innovations, but the originators of these ideas, among others, put the blame instead on the legendary conservatism of the classical music world. Luthiers such as the Parisian Daniel Friedrich have worked with acoustic engineers to come up with less radical and more convincing results. Friedrich conducted innumerable experiments with different types of braces, all of them scientifically documented and filed. These instruments—all with high standards, yet each with its subtle differences—together prove that there is not one definitive type of bracing but rather as many acceptable variations as there are individual luthiers, or woods with different characteristics, or clients with contradictory needs.

Another important change occurred after World War II, when nylon strings were adopted by almost all classical and flamenco musicians. Up until then, strings were made of gut, or of metal for other types of music. This innovation, which originated in New York, allowed musicians to play on strings that were more consistent, more durable, and considerably less expensive.

Jeronimo Peña Guitar (1978)

This beautiful guitar with decorative rosette is the work of the Spanish luthier Jeronimo Peña. Made of rosewood and cedar, it has an exceptionally long scale length of 26 1/3 inches. Ramírez was the first luthier to abandon the 25 1/2-inch scale length established by Torres, when he built instruments with a 26-1/4-inch span for Segovia. Today's guitars have returned to a more reasonable length, and in fact many teachers advise their younger students, or those with small hands, to opt for a 25-inch scale length.

Kazuo Sato Guitar (1995)

The Japanese school of guitar making, pioneered by Masaru Kohno, is still alive and well today. Sato, a Japanese luthier based in Germany, is part of a new wave of Japanese craftsmen dedicated to creating personal and innovative models. Thanks to artisans such as Sato, the inaccurate stereotype of the Japanese luthier as a skilled but uninspired imitator is beginning to be dispelled.

George Lowden Guitar

This instrument, built by the Irish luthier George Lowden, is unusual in that it features a cedar table. This wood, which was once used in the construction of vihuelas, was revived for guitar construction by José Ramírez III in the 1960s. Ramírez even declared at that time that Stradivarius himself would have used cedar had it been available during his era. Although this opinion is not shared by many luthiers, cedar does have a reputation for increasing bass tones and for producing a soft and velvety, if sometimes imprecise, sound.

The Flamenco Guitar

A Grand Spanish Tradition

**Maurice Dupont
Flamenco Guitar**

This instrument, though built in Cognac by French luthier Maurice Dupont, features all the characteristics of the Spanish flamenco guitar: a cypress body, and a spruce soundboard complete with golpeador between the bridge and the soundhole. This plate provides protection for the instrument as the musician strikes its surface rhythmically as he plays. The peghead is also typical of this type of instrument.

Flamenco, whose roots go back as far as antiquity, is a genre that originated in Andalusia. It combines three equally important elements: singing, dancing, and guitar playing. This rich and rhythmically complex musical style has appeared in many forms over the years. Like the blues, flamenco was born of the hardships and misery of the people of a particular region, but has since attracted a worldwide audience thanks to internationally known artists such as guitarist Paco de Lucía.

tante opened in Seville in 1842. The proliferation of these establishments better enabled flamenco artists to support themselves through their music—that is, until they started to gradually disappear in the 1920s.

Flamenco unfortunately started losing some of its authenticity as its audience widened to those unfamiliar with the genre. The influence of show business, as it often does, began to dilute the original tradition: first, castanets made an appearance; then guitarists, not to be upstaged, began to entertain their audiences with

He has pushed the boundaries of flamenco to new limits, much to the displeasure of many of his more traditional colleagues. Having been inspired by diverse musical styles, he justifies his philosophy: "Flamenco has too much character and emotional power to remain static forever." The distinctive qualities of flamenco are its use of a particular scale, the Phrygian mode, and its North African influences which can be traced back to the Moorish invasions that took place toward the end of the first millennium. Flamenco also possesses traces of Indian music, such as the use of intervals inferior to the half step (a peculiarity also found in the blues).

Flamenco first spread throughout Andalusia, then to the greater part of Spain, thanks to the advent of cafés cantantes, a sort of cabaret devoted entirely to this genre. The first café can-

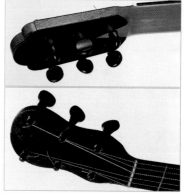

**Flamenco (above)
and Romantic (below) Pegheads**

Contrary to popular opinion, the flamenco guitar is not just a variation of the classical model. Both instruments do have a common ancestor—though the modern flamenco guitar most resembles the nineteenth-century instruments that spawned them both. For example, the pegheads of flamenco guitars are not slotted like those of classical guitars, but are carved from a solid piece of wood into which ebony pegs are fitted and adjusted by simple friction.

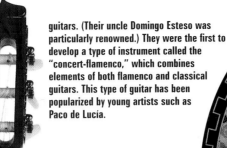

Hermanos Conde Flamenco Guitar (1994)

The Conde brothers, based in Madrid, are the third generation in a family of luthiers specializing in the construction of flamenco guitars. (Their uncle Domingo Esteso was particularly renowned.) They were the first to develop a type of instrument called the "concert-flamenco," which combines elements of both flamenco and classical guitars. This type of guitar has been popularized by young artists such as Paco de Lucía.

stunts like playing with gloves or socks over their hands. In spite of all this, survival, if not fortune, would be flamenco's destiny.

Just as humble guitarists from the delta moved north to seek fame in and around Chicago, poor musicians from southern Spain were arriving en masse to settle in Madrid. It was about this time that Ramón Montoya (1880–1949) established the foundations of the modern fla-

menco guitar. In the 1950s, the style became increasingly popularity in foreign countries as artists such as Perico el del Lunar and Roman el Granaino exported an art form that was more appreciated in South America and English-speaking countries than it was in its native Spain. Today, artists such as Paco Peña or Paco de Lucía have taken over where they left off.

Once again, it was Torres who gave the modern flamenco guitar its outline

shape, with a smaller body and lighter construction.

Models made by Torres often had five braces (most contemporary builders use seven), and the fingerboard was often built of rosewood rather than ebony, which further reduced the instrument's weight. This pared-down construction, probably conceived for reasons of economy, also had the advantage of producing very resonant guitars with a volume that could stand out in the midst of a musical mêlée—that is, they could successfully compete with the powerful voices of the singers and the forceful footsteps of the flamenco dancers.

Also found on flamenco guitars is a protective plate next to the soundhole on the treble side, and sometimes on the bass side as well. This piece of plastic or tortoise shell, called the golpeador, protects the face of the guitar as the player strikes and taps the instrument, a practice that is an essential part of the flamenco genre.

The most renowned flamenco luthiers are from Spain: Santos Hernández (1873–1942), Domingo Esteso (1882–1937), Marcelo Barbero (1904–1955), and more recently, Manuel Reyes in Cordova and the Conde

brothers in Madrid.

Elsewhere, there are fewer luthiers specializing in flamenco than in classical guitars, yet there are some talented craftsmen in the United States, like Dennis Hill or Benito Huipe, or in France, like Maurice Dupont.

Cypress

Flamenco guitars are often made of cypress, an inexpensive wood that is readily available in Spain. Cypress can be milled into very thin boards, which can significantly reduce the overall weight of the finished instrument.

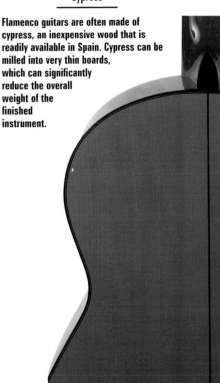

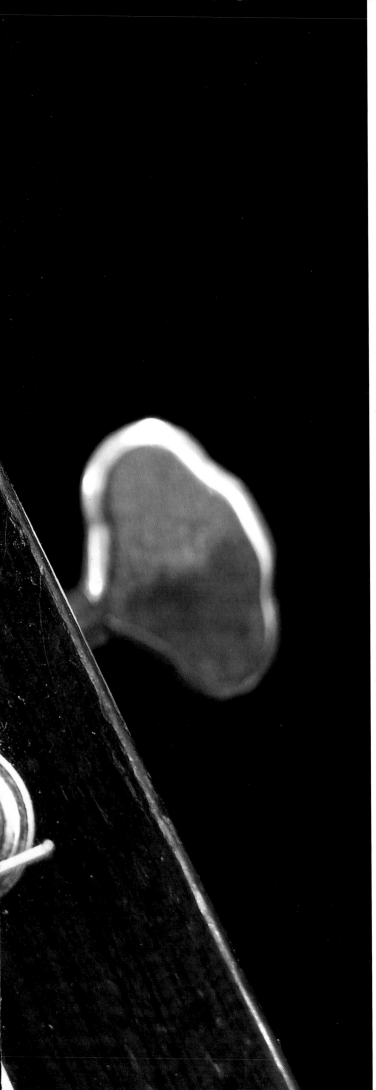

Martin: The Definitive ∼ Acoustic ∼ Guitar

Americans have a fascination with dynasties—even though our "royal families" rule over oil fields and fast-food emporiums rather than kingdoms, and our "palaces" are Wall Street skyscrapers and Silicon Valley offices. The Martin family of guitar fame can certainly be counted among these American-style dynasties. Furthermore, they possess the required elements of the classic American success story: an immigrant ancestor who escaped the narrow-mindedness of the Old World, followed by generations of heirs, some very successful and some less so. As with all dynasties, some Martin descendants carried the family torch with pride, and others simply coasted along, contributing little to the legacy. Remarkably, a century and a half after its inception, the Martin company is still run by a direct descendant of the founder, a unique case in the American instrument industry. In fact, Martin is probably one of the oldest family-owned businesses of any kind in the country.

The modern Martin facilities have little in common with the modest workshop of its pioneering days. And today, unlike in years past, market demands largely dictate the direction of the company. Furthermore, like many other corporations, Martin has had to relocate part of its operations. Yet Martin is still known as a company with a heart, one that produces handmade instruments of high standards, and one with a mission to satisfy its clientele. For all these reasons, an ever-growing number of musicians dream of owning their very own Martin—the Rolls Royce of acoustic guitars.

The Martin logo, placed on the headstock, has always been a mark of quality.

The Martin Dynasty

Five Generations of Guitar Makers

In 1833, as Europe was about to experience the Torres guitar revolution, a German citizen by the name of Christian Friedrich Martin, along with many of his fellow countrymen, boarded a ship that would take him to the United States of America.

Prior to C.F. Martin, numerous Europeans had made a similar voyage, guided by their faith and forced out by religious persecution in the Old World. These willing expatriates were attracted by the spirit of tolerance and dynamism that was flourishing in the new country.

It was for a similar, if less spiritual, reason that C.F. Martin became a candidate for exodus: the members of the overly powerful Violin Makers' Guild, who considered themselves the only qualified instruments craftsmen, treated guitars with condescension. Martin was apprenticed in the 1820s to Johann Stauffer, a renowned Viennese guitar luthier, and the first instruments he built in America, starting in 1833 in his small New York shop on Hudson Street, were similar in many ways to the ones crafted by his former master. Especially similar was the peghead of the instrument, with its sinuous profile and all six tuning keys on one side.

Martin, like many recent immigrants, had trouble adjusting to his new life, despite earnest efforts on his part to assimilate. (He even anglicized his name to Christian Frederick Martin.) In 1838, on the advice of his fellow émigrés who were also ill at ease in their adopted city, he decided

Christian Friedrich Martin

Once an apprentice of Stauffer, C.F. Martin left his native Germany for the United States in 1833. Here he founded what would one day become one of the largest guitar manufacturing companies in the world.

to relocate to Pennsylvania, where the rolling hillsides reminded him of his homeland.

He set up his first shop in the little town of Nazareth, in the very place where the modern

Martin factory operates today. Like his former European colleagues, Martin at that time was fond of using rare materials like ivory and mother-of-pearl, and he had a preference for elegantly decorated instruments. Martin soon realized, however, that he would have to change his style if he wanted to be successful in his new home: Americans at that time, mostly white and Protestant, were modest, hard-working, practical people with little time for pomp and circumstance. Martin therefore decided to simplify the design of his instruments as much as possible, although he never sacrificed his trademark standard of quality, his attention to detail, or his impeccable craftsmanship.

This parallel mission, the pursuit of structural perfection balanced with aesthetic sobriety, has endured throughout the history of the company and remains alive and well today. (It is interesting to note that Pennsylvania was also home to the Shakers, whose spartan furniture is highly appreciated today for the same kind of elegant simplicity that made Martin guitars famous.)

C.F. Martin also gave up the Stauffer-style peghead for a more classic rectangular shape. Similarly, his ornate bridges, reminiscent of European "mustache" bridges, slowly gave way to rectangular ones. These simple bridges were adorned by two pyramids sculpted on each side, an embellishment that remained on Martin guitars until the end of the 1920s. Decoration was also reduced to a bare mini-

C.F. Martin Jr.

C. F. Martin was blessed by the birth of a son on October 2, 1825, while he was still working for Stauffer in Vienna. C. F. Jr. played only a minor role in the development of the family business from 1860 until his death in 1988.

C.F. Martin III

The career of C.F. Martin III, born in 1894, was much like that of his brother, H.K. Martin—both were overshadowed by the personality of their father, Frank Henry Martin. He did, however, have the distinction of running the company, together with his son Herbert, during the 1960s and 1970s, which were its peak production years.

mum, with only a simple rosewood or ivory border along the body, or else the herringbone border that is still found on twentieth-century models. Martin also gradually increased the size of his instruments—particularly the lower bout—while narrowing the waist, giving them a shape more or less like that of the classical guitars that were also evolving back in Europe.

Frank Henry Martin

Born on October 14, 1866, the son of C.F. Martin Jr. found himself at the helm of the family business at the young age of twenty two, following his father's death. He played a significant role in the development of the company, and was responsible for the creation of most of the legendary models from the 1920s and 1930s. He retired in 1945, three years before his death.

Martin in the Nineteenth Century

The Birth of the X-Brace

While Torres and other Spanish luthiers were establishing the rules of classical guitar construction, C.F. Martin was working on the foundations of what would later become the prototypical American steel-string acoustic guitar—a style universally known and duplicated today. His most revolutionary innovation was the now famous "X-brace."

Torres had proven that fan-braced tops allowed classical guitars (equipped with gut, and later nylon, strings) to resonate to their full potential. Martin, simultaneously, elaborated on a new system, whose value was especially appreciated eighty years later when steel strings started appearing. This system was composed of two main diagonal braces that crossed each other between the bridge and the soundhole. Known as "X-bracing," Martin's system was stronger than the one proposed by Torres, but was probably less suited to the gut strings used in those days. In developing this pattern, Martin, pragmatic as always, was probably considering the rough and tumble way of life of most Americans at that time. When

the use of steel strings became common in the 1930s, X-bracing proved itself to be wonderfully efficient, offering a balanced compromise between strength (steel strings put much more pressure on the bridge than do gut strings) and the freedom of vibration a soundboard requires.

Martin was still a family business then, and the instruments built by the company during the nineteenth century are today much rarer than its contemporaries, such as Washburns, which were issued from production lines by the thousands.

Martin 2-27 (ca. 1870)

With its rosewood body, ebony bridge and fingerboard, mother-of-pearl crown that surrounds the soundhole, and multicolored herringbone inlay that borders the top, this is among the most ornate Martin guitars of this era. This early guitar, still in marvelous condition, was already equipped with Martin's now-famous X-bracing, which was a feature on all their guitars from the 1850s onward. The size of this guitar, which may seem relatively conservative today, was quite impressive at the time, considering that such instruments were most often played at home or for small audiences. These instruments, in fact, were often referred to as "parlor guitars."

X-bracing

The renowned X-bracing system, first conceived by C.F. Martin, is clearly visible on this internal view of a modern guitar soundboard. The main bracing is made up of two braces that intersect between the soundhole and the bridge.

Up until 1939, the brace's crossing point was located just below the soundhole, leaving a larger surface of vibrating board. This design was modified in the interests of strength, and the intersection was again brought down to a more central position. The placement of the secondary braces was often determined by trial and error, in an attempt to allow the soundboard to achieve its optimal acoustic potential. The braces on this soundboard are rather thick—a typical design in modern guitar construction. Up until 1944, Martin actually thinned out his guitars' braces (and called these "scalloped braces") to allow for freer soundboard vibration. Unfortunately, this practice had to be abandoned as it tended to make his instruments somewhat more fragile and therefore less practical for the musicians of the day who were in the habit of over-tightening the strings in an effort to increase their volume. Today, Martin is reissuing a number of models with scalloped braces.

The piece of wood pierced with six holes located under the apex of the cross is called the bridge plate. Its function is to reinforce the table under the bridge and to help the strings stay in place once wound. The strings, in fact, have small balls at the ends that are supported by this plate, which therefore prevents wear and damage to the soundboard. Martin's bridge plates were made of maple up until 1968. Since then, Martin switched to rosewood (seen on the model pictured here), only to gradually return to the use of maple starting in 1976.

Martin 2-27 peghead

Martin abandoned his early scrolled pegheads, inherited from Stauffer in the 1840s, in favor of slotted heads like this one, similar to those on classical guitars. The tuning pegs, like the binding, were made of natural ivory, a material that the Martin company has not used since 1918.

The Martin 45 Series

Superlative Decoration

As early as 1852, Martin offered a catalog of guitars in standard sizes numbered from 0 to 5 (0, paradoxically being the largest, and 5, the smallest). Soon after, the company also started using a numerical suffix that informed the client as to the level of ornamentation on a specific instrument. C.F. Martin also put to use the managerial experience he gained while heading Stauffer's workshop to optimize his own company's business plan. Capitalizing on the economic growth of his adopted country, the advent of new markets, and the expansion of the railways, he succeeded in distributing his instruments throughout the whole country and slowly turned his small family business into a nation-wide enterprise.

After his death in 1873, the founder was replaced by his son C.F. Martin Jr., who had a lesser role in the expansion of the company. However, C.F. Jr.'s son, Frank Henry, played an important part in the growth of the business, taking several risks that were to paypaid off in the long run.

The future did not look bright for the American guitar: its popularity was waning in favor of the banjo and the mandolin. Frank Henry therefore decided to begin making mandolins. This decision led to a falling out with Zoebisch, Martin's original distributor, who had no confidence in the new product, and Frank Henry saw this disagreement as an opportunity to establish his own distribution network. In 1902 he also decided to launch a 15-inch model, called the

"000," hoping the increased volume of the instrument would help it compete with the powerful and popular banjo. Paradoxically, it was the Martin mandolins of this era, considered rather mediocre by today's connoisseurs, that were then highly popular. On the other hand, the 000 model, revered by modern players, was a complete failure, and it was not until the 1920s and the advent of steel strings that this superb model was finally fully appreciated.

Frank Henry Martin took another chance by breaking away from the conservative tradition of the company. He paid close attention to his competitors, such as Washburn and its subsidiary, Lyon & Healy, who were at that time successfully marketing highly ornate instruments. Martin decided to jump aboard that trend, but did so gradually and cautiously, applying a mother-of-pearl rosette on a few models starting in 1850, then adding some inlays on the fingerboard. Finally, in 1904, Martin guitars were fully ornamented with mother-of-pearl borders around the table, soundhole, fingerboard, back, and rim, as well as with intricate inlays on the fingerboard and peghead. This line of instruments, known as the "45" line, is still today the most ornate of the company. Despite their aesthetic appeal, it was not until the 1920s, that opulent decade of carefree living and easy cash, that these instruments found the affluent clientele they needed. The success of the 45s was to be short-lived, however, due to the economic decline that struck America after the stock market crash of 1929.

Martin 0-45 (1929)

The 45 models made before the interruption of the series in 1942 are extremely rare and highly coveted by collectors. Only 158 guitars like this one were produced by Martin between 1904 and 1939. Like all 45 guitars, this instrument features mother-of-pearl inlay around the soundhole, top, back, and sides.

0-45 Slotted Peghead

The peghead of this instrument is still slotted and resembles that of a classical guitar. It is decorated with a "torch inlay" motif, which was found on all 45 models until 1934. After that date, the motif was replaced by a vertical, mother-of-pearl company logo, quite different from the discrete decal Martin generally used.

0-45 Soundhole

The mother-of-pearl inlays is all done by hand. The craftsmen who specialize in this type of work must first select pieces of mother-of-pearl that are similar in color and texture. These are then cut into several pieces that must be arranged with extreme precision to create the illusion that the border is made of one single piece.

0-45 Fingerboard

This ebony fingerboard is bordered with an ivoroid, a synthetic material that resembles ivory. As on all post-1914 Martin guitars, the fingerboard features eight "snowflake" inlays. It is interesting to note that all Martin instruments up to 1934 have rectangular frets. After that date, the company switched to T-section frets, which have rounded edges to make guitar-playing more comfortable.

0-45 Back

The back and rims, or sides, of this instrument—like all 45 models of the day—were built from a high-grade Brazilian rosewood. This wood, now quite rare, combines both excellent acoustic and exceptional aesthetic properties, and often has a beautifully patterned grain, more so than the Indian rosewood commonly used today. Also notice the central "zipper" inlay, typical of 45s of that period.

From 12 to 14 Frets
The End of the Banjo's Reign

D-28 (1933)

This guitar is rare for two reasons. Firstly, it is a 12-fret slotted peghead D-28, and Martin only produced around 40 such instruments between 1931 and 1934. Secondly, this guitar displays a shaded top. Martin did not start using these sunburst finishes on its guitars until 1931, and it remained a rare feature. This guitar—part of the impressive collection that belongs to guitar expert Gary Burnette and once belonged to guitarist Norman Blake—might be the only one of its kind that combines these two characteristics.

Over time, the small-sized Martins were gradually replaced by larger instruments, sizes 0 to 000 being especially popular until the beginning of the 1930s. In those days, guitars were often built of rosewood; beginning in 1906, however, Martin used mahogany for the construction of its instruments. Mahogany had thus far been neglected by the vast majority of luthiers, who considered it inferior, but around this time its acoustic characteristics—such as brightness and balance—were starting to become recognized. It was also at the beginning of the 1920s that Martin began to conceive of a guitar capable of resisting the added tension of steel strings (a problem that Gibson had solved almost twenty years earlier). In 1922, the company offered the first model with a mahogany soundboard built for this purpose; by the end of the decade, all Martin models would emerge from the factory with soundboards and braces designed to withstand the extra tension of steel strings. Once again, Mar-

tin's motivation was to compete with the power of other manufacturers' guitars, as well as with that of the banjo which, in spite of a decline in popularity, still dominated the sound of the jazz bands of the day. Martin was looking for the ultimate solution that would turn die-hard banjo players into aspiring guitar players and therefore potential clients. To this end, the company started to take a close look at the specific habits the kept banjo players from converting to the guitar.

The banjo, for instance, had a narrower neck and smaller body size, which made the upper part of the fingerboard more accessible. Martin guitars, with their traditional 12-fret necks, were not likely to attract potential defectors. Under the tutelage of Perry Bechtel, a then renowned Atlanta banjo player, Martin created a guitar with a longer scale and a narrower neck that joined the body at the fourteenth fret. This instrument, called the "OM" or "orchestral model," was the link to the modern flat-top steel-string acoustic guitar. The guitars in the first OM series, launched in 1929 and consisting of the 18, 28, 45, and 45 Deluxe, were fitted with banjo tuners perpendicular to the peghead, a final tribute to a vanishing instrument. With the OM, Martin also returned to the large rectangular-shaped peghead that they had often used in the nineteenth century and had later abandoned in favor of a slotted-style one.

0-18 (1933), 00-18 (1932), 000-18 (1945)

These three guitar sizes, which might seem small by today's standards, were at the time of their respective launches the largest of the Martin line. The 0 model, with its 13 1/2 inch body-size, appeared in 1854. Model 00, at 14 1/2 inches, entered the picture in 1877. The 000, at 15 inches, came out in 1902 and remained the largest Martin model for a long while. These three guitars,

OM-28 (1930)

OM models, which were only available from 1929 to 1934, were the first Martin guitars with a 14-fret neck. They were also the first ones to appear with a celluloid pickguard. Applied on the soundboard under the treble side of the soundhole, the purpose of the pickguard was to protect the instrument from the pick strokes of the musician. The pickguard on this model is quite small, characteristic of the first year of production. It would be enlarged the following year. With the OM models, Martin also returned to a rectangular solid-shaped peghead, similar to the ones built by the company in the nineteenth century. Notice that there is no Martin decal on the peghead; this feature was to appear only from 1932 on.

all of style 18 (that is, made of mahogany), have interesting differences. The first two have a sunburst finish, a new option started in 1931 on the Martin line. The 00-18, made in 1932, still has a 12-fret neck and a slotted head. On the other hand, the 0-18, built the following year, features a 14-fret neck. (It was the first model after the OM to feature this option.)

The Pre-War Years

Martin's Golden Era

With the advent of the 1930s came the production of Martin's famed Dreadnought model, with a wider soundbox that would provide more volume and exceptional bass response. This model became the standard that most acoustic folk guitars have tried to match ever since. To design this instrument, Frank Henry Martin drew inspiration from a prototype that the Martin company had produced in a very limited number for the Ditson company of Boston back in 1916. Martin launched the new model in 1931 and named it D (for *Dreadnought*, a World War I battleship).

Curiously, the first Dreadnoughts still had 12-fret necks and slotted heads, but beginning in 1934, Martin offered the first D-18, D-28, and D-45 guitars with 14-fret necks and solid heads. The 14-fret Dreadnought produced by Martin soon became the industry standard, emulated by all the competitors. In their attempts to rival these remarkable guitars, some competitors, like Gibson with its Advanced Jumbo, even came close to surpassing them.

In later years, the Martin Company would look back upon its glorious past and try in vain to recapture the qualities of their legendary instruments from the 1930s. What was the secret, if any, and what characteristics distinguished these outstanding guitars? Was it the quality of the materials, or perhaps the extreme care that was applied to their construction? Was it age that improved them? Or did the secret come from the braces, the vital center of any acoustic guitar?

Indeed, on the early Dreadnoughts, Martin used a specific X-bracing system: one with a cross-section located very close to the soundhole, leaving an especially large surface of vibrating soundboard. These instruments were amazingly powerful. Unfortunately, such guitars were also relatively frail, and Martin had to give up this feature in 1939, relocating the braces to a more moderate position. At the same time, each individual brace was scalloped by hand to keep the guitar light and in the interests of optimal vibration. Then, at the end of 1944, Martin again had to alter its bracing system because of clients who persisted in using strings of damaging gauges. Martin did, however, revive the scalloped bracing system in the 1980s on a few specific models, thanks to the demand of a better-educated public and a growing number of vintage guitar enthusiasts. Martin models from the 1930s are especially coveted today by musicians, who can rarely afford them, and by collectors, who will pay premium prices for those in good original condition. The D-45, of which only ninety-one examples were built between 1933 and 1942,

D-18 (1937)

Built the same year as the herringbone models displayed on the next page (a magical year for many Martin enthusiasts), this D-18 model differs mainly from a D-28 of the same vintage in that it has a mahogany body and has no herringbone trim along the soundboard. On the model to the left, the herringbone marquetry is replaced by a faux tortoise-shell plastic binding—a material used by Martin since 1936.

D-18 (1944)

A few structural details distinguish this D-18 model from the previous one. The main difference, as far as musicians are concerned, lies in the width of the neck at the nut, which considerably decreased in mid-1939. Also, restrictions caused by the war forced Martin to reinforce the neck with a piece of ebony rather than with their former metal truss rods. For similar reasons, the tuning pegs on this guitar are plastic. Together, these features make the Dreadnoughts of this period (1942–1944) very light instruments that are highly regarded by many musicians.

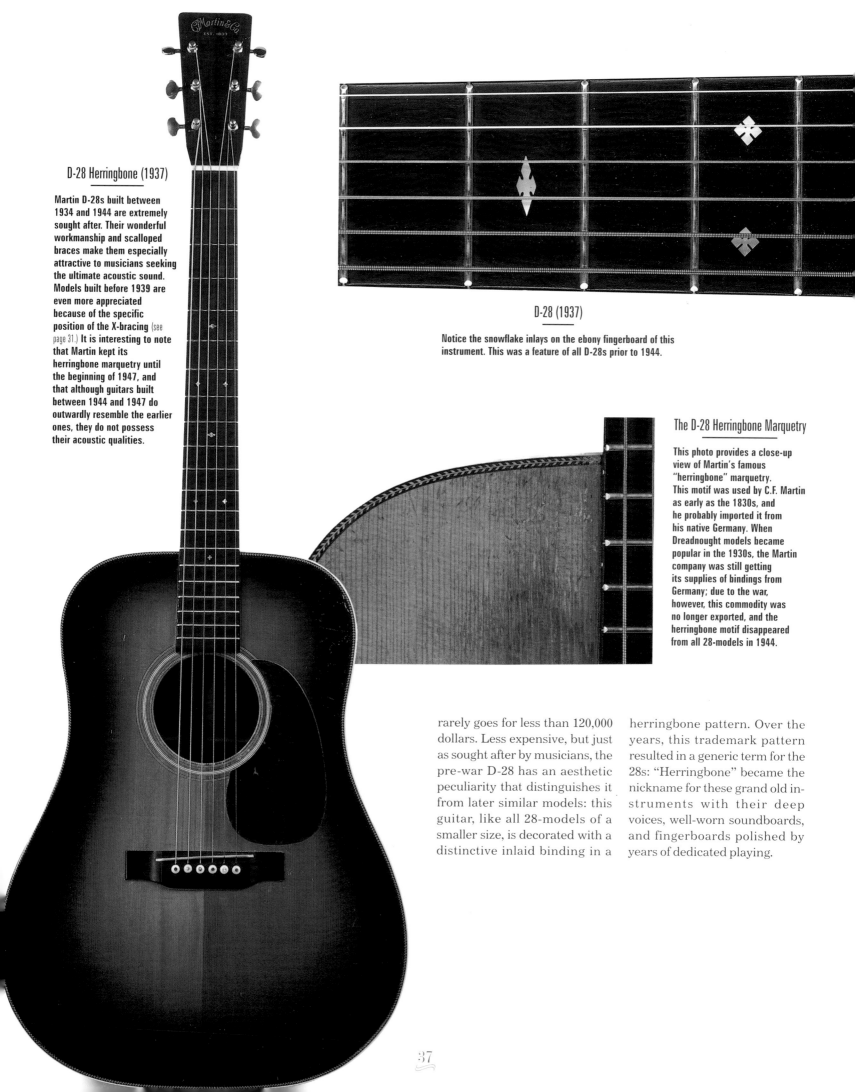

D-28 Herringbone (1937)

Martin D-28s built between 1934 and 1944 are extremely sought after. Their wonderful workmanship and scalloped braces make them especially attractive to musicians seeking the ultimate acoustic sound. Models built before 1939 are even more appreciated because of the specific position of the X-bracing (see page 31.) It is interesting to note that Martin kept its herringbone marquetry until the beginning of 1947, and that although guitars built between 1944 and 1947 do outwardly resemble the earlier ones, they do not possess their acoustic qualities.

D-28 (1937)

Notice the snowflake inlays on the ebony fingerboard of this instrument. This was a feature of all D-28s prior to 1944.

The D-28 Herringbone Marquetry

This photo provides a close-up view of Martin's famous "herringbone" marquetry. This motif was used by C.F. Martin as early as the 1830s, and he probably imported it from his native Germany. When Dreadnought models became popular in the 1930s, the Martin company was still getting its supplies of bindings from Germany; due to the war, however, this commodity was no longer exported, and the herringbone motif disappeared from all 28-models in 1944.

rarely goes for less than 120,000 dollars. Less expensive, but just as sought after by musicians, the pre-war D-28 has an aesthetic peculiarity that distinguishes it from later similar models: this guitar, like all 28-models of a smaller size, is decorated with a distinctive inlaid binding in a herringbone pattern. Over the years, this trademark pattern resulted in a generic term for the 28s: "Herringbone" became the nickname for these grand old instruments with their deep voices, well-worn soundboards, and fingerboards polished by years of dedicated playing.

Martin Today
A Return to the Quality

The quality of Martin guitars began to noticeably and steadily decline from the end of the war up until the late 1970s. Although the company remained an industry leader and its name continued to be associated with quality, in reality, it had slowly slipped away from the high standards of construction that it had maintained until the 1940s. This change was due to several factors.

First, the reinforced bracing system referred to earlier, as well as attempts at building instruments with an overall sturdier structure, led to a significant decline in acoustic attributes. Musical quality was often compromised for the sake of added strength. Martin was one of the rare companies to offer a lifetime guarantee to the original owner, and, paradoxically, it may have been the fear of seeing the guitars sent back to the factory that hastened its downfall.

Another key to the decline in quality was that all major builders were having a hard time locating high-quality wood, and certain varieties simply disappeared from the market. Thus, Adirondack spruce, which the company had been using for its soundboards before the war because of its remarkable acoustic qualities, was replaced by sitka, a softer wood. As for the wonderfully resonant Brazilian rosewood, it became so expensive that Martin had to discontinue using it in 1969. Today, its export is totally banned by international conventions, and it has been largely replaced by Indian rosewood, which some luthiers consider inferior.

The changes in quality might also be attributed to the effect of the baby-boomer generation that invaded the musical market of the 1960s. Followers of musical styles that were mainly guitar-based, this new wave of dedicated clients caused Martin and their competitors to boost their productions to an extreme. The increased activity in Nazareth's workshops inevitably led to a decline in craftsmanship.

D-45 Custom (1993)

In 1993, Martin built fifty of these exceptionally ornamented D-45s. This guitar, number 11 of the series, not only showcases traditional mother-of-pearl around the soundboard, back, and sides, but also features intricate inlay on the bridge and pickguard. It also has a tree-of-life motif on the fingerboard, reminiscent of the ones found on parlor guitars of the late nineteenth century (see pages 64-65).

The Martin factory set production records at the beginning of the 1970s, but this commercially rewarding period would not continue indefinitely. By the middle of the decade, production started to drop, and Martin had to deal with the first workers' strike in its long history. This resilient company, however, knew how to cope. Encouraged by the requests of knowledgeable clients unable to afford original pre-war instruments, Martin turned to its own past and started making new guitars that possessed the characteristics of its legendary instruments from the 1930s. As early as 1976, a "Herring-bone" with scalloped braces, called the HD-28, was released, soon followed by numerous other quality reissues. In 1979, the company opened its Custom Shop, a combination old-fashioned workshop and experimental lab that filled special orders and customized instruments, adding a human touch to their otherwise mass production operation. Then in 1981, Martin caused a mini-revolution by offering a cutaway on some of its models. This notch on the upper bout of the body, trebleward, allows the left hand of the player to explore previously untouched areas of the fingerboard. In the 1980s, under the direction of C.F. Martin IV, the current president of the company, a series of new models appeared. One example is the J (or Jumbo) model, the largest guitar currently produced by the company.

000 C-16 (1992)

A new revolution occurred in 1981 when Martin introduced the "cutaway." This notch in the guitar body allows access to the treble end of the fingerboard. The model pictured here, launched in 1990, uses the classic 15-inch size of the 000. Also noteworthy is its unusual oval soundhole, as well as its scalloped braces which Martin gradually started to reintroduce in 1976 after having phased them out in 1944.

Jumbo Custom Sunburst (1985)

Under the influence of C.F. Martin IV, the current president of the company, a series of new guitars appeared in the 1980s. One of these is the J (or Jumbo) model, presently the largest of the company. This guitar, with its mother-of-pearl bindings (similar to those on the 41-model) and its beautiful sunburst finish, is particularly ornate.

The Martin Catalog

Today, Martin has returned to the quality of yesteryear, and its comprehensive catalog offers a wide selection of reissue models. The instruments they currently build might very well one day rival those produced in the glorious 1930s.

The Gibson Saga
~ A Century ~
of Innovation

Of all modern guitar manufacturers, Gibson is certainly the most diversified, and its influence has been felt in a great many domains. Its electric guitars are the most famous and are used by rock musicians all over the world, but arch-top Gibsons can also be found in the hands of the finest jazz musicians. As for acoustic guitars, Gibson has been the only serious threat to Martin's supremacy in this area over the years. As if that weren't enough, Gibson also built lap-steels, banjos, and mandolins while paying outstanding care to detail. Even more remarkable is the fact that, despite this flood of products, the company rarely fell short of its reputation for superior craftsmanship. Guitar lovers—who, incidentally, are often automobile enthusiasts as well—like to compare Gibson to a car manufacturer that simultaneously produces excellent luxury limos, family sedans, ATVs, race cars, and motorbikes!

The guitar has evolved immensely since the beginning of this century, and much of its evolution can be attributed to the luthiers and engineers of this renowned company. These expert craftsmen often followed the path set by their illustrious founder: Orville Gibson, a creative, likable, and entirely unique character. Together with Martin, Gibson set the standards for modern acoustic guitar construction and has since inspired numerous other manufacturers.

Instruments made by Gibson today combine the classic designs of yesteryear with thoroughly modern construction methods.

Orville Gibson

Legendary Figure and Genius Luthier

Julius Bellson published *The Gibson Story* in 1973.

When Orville Gibson first crafted odd-shaped guitars in his Kalamazoo workshop, his friends probably never imagined that instruments bearing his name would still be enthusiastically played by decibel-crashing rock bands more than a century later. It's possible, though, that he might have imagined it! In light of his life story and accomplishments, Orville Gibson was not only as an obviously talented luthier, but also as a true visionary. The innovations he devised, many of them still in use today, clearly demonstrate that he, unlike C.F. Martin, was not only a meticulous and rigorous craftsman, but also a veritable artist inspired by a boundless imagination and a creative spirit that occasionally bordered on delirium.

Born in 1856 in upstate New York, Orville H. Gibson settled down in the little town of Kalamazoo, Michigan, in the early 1880s. He worked at odd jobs that allowed him free time to pursue his true passion: guitar making. Eventually, in 1896, he opened a small shop of his own.

Orville Gibson was not an ordinary character. In the old sepia prints, he is usually surrounded by an odd assortment of objects and ornaments that create cheerful, exotic settings which are always strangely tempered by his serious posture and often tortured expression. The man was visibly consumed by his passion.

In these early years, Gibson was building guitars and mandolins with a unique look that eventually attracted the attention of five local businessmen. According to legend, these five initial investors took advantage of their new partner's bohemian spirit and persuaded him to sign a contract that today might seem disadvantageous. There was a 2,500 dollars remuneration to Gibson, which was quite a sum of money back then, but, to put it in context, we must remember that this amount is far from enough to even acquire one of his own instruments today. Orville Gibson was said to have been gradually pushed away from the supervision of what was to become a real factory. The real story is probably much less dramatic. Gibson, like many artists that belie the common cliché, was actually perfectly capable of protecting his own interests in business matters. The clauses in the contract seem, in fact, to be those of a real partnership, and Gibson most likely voluntarily distanced himself from the business end of things. This might have been because he was disappointed in the results of mass production and worried about the integrity of his original concepts. It is also conceivable that in the face of his increased psychological problems, he was encouraged to take advantage of the comfortable pension his contract guaranteed him. Whatever the reason, after the partnership was formed, he no longer played a major role in the development of the company. Regularly hospitalized after 1909, Gibson eventually moved to Ogdensburg, New York, where he died on August 21, 1918. By that time, the Gibson company was already a flourishing enterprise. Cleverly exploiting the mandolin fad at that time, the company's board of directors succeeded in popularizing the new models conceived by Orville Gibson. Throughout its history, the Gibson company, often ahead of its time, would remain true to the creative spirit of its founder and would contribute enormously to the conception of the modern American guitar.

Orville Gibson

Orville Gibson came from a family of artists. His father, John Gibson, British by birth, was an art enthusiast, and all of Orville's siblings pursued artistic careers. Orville himself always applied a creative flair to instrument construction, improvising new techniques, many of which have gone down in history.

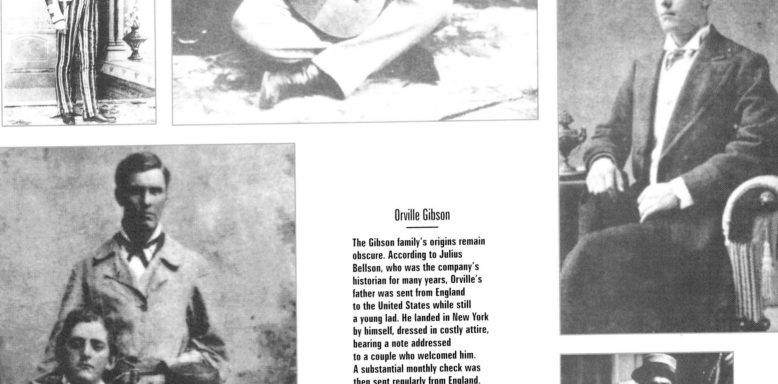

Orville Gibson

The Gibson family's origins remain obscure. According to Julius Bellson, who was the company's historian for many years, Orville's father was sent from England to the United States while still a young lad. He landed in New York by himself, dressed in costly attire, bearing a note addressed to a couple who welcomed him. A substantial monthly check was then sent regularly from England. These funds, which gave him the means to raise a large family, continued to arrive until his death. Despite much research, the genealogy of this opulent British family remains unknown.

The Early Years

The Influence of Classical Lutherie

Orville Gibson's basic idea was to apply the unique principles of violin construction to the construction of guitars and mandolins. Up until his time, guitars and mandolins were built with a perfectly planed spruce soundboard (with the exception of a few French and Italian instruments that had boards with two angled surfaces). Gibson came up with the idea of carving his guitar and mandolin tops from relatively thicker pieces of wood, resulting in a convex surface on top of which was placed a moveable bridge. Strings were no longer attached to the bridge, but rather to the end of the guitar by way of a tailpiece. This system, very similar to the one used for violin construction, radically transformed the acoustic function of the guitar and gave it a completely different type of sound.

The result seemed to please the musicians of the day, since Gibson's instruments quickly gained an ever-growing popularity. His success might also have been attributed to the distinct profile and aesthetic quality of all of his models. Unlike most luthiers of the day, who favored modest ornamentation, Gibson let his passionate imagination lead the way, and he adorned his instruments with complex mother-of-pearl inlays, intricate marquetry, and spectacular scrolls.

Curiously, Gibson did not apply for a patent for most of his inventions; the only copyright he secured concerned a strange method of carving the sides of an instrument from a solid piece of wood—a practice which did not outlast him. (Guitar sides are generally built from thin layers of wood that are curved to the desired shape under

Artist-Model Mandolin (1906)

This instrument is typical of the first models built by Gibson at the beginning of the century, notably because of its dark finish, scroll, three points, and oval soundhole. The extended fingerboard as well as the pickguard were set directly on the soundboard and decorated with intricate mother-of-pearl motifs. This mandolin, built from walnut, disappeared from the Gibson catalog in 1908.

heat action.) After the founder departed, Gibson's executives made some wise selections between his more spectacular inventions and those with less promise. They of course retained the Gibson soundboard construction method, as well as the scrolls which were found on his O-model guitars and F-model mandolins. Similarly, colorful finishes, of which Orville was fond, were maintained on the Gibson line. Black and orange, in particular, were often found on instruments of that period. Improvements were made regularly during the first months of the company's existence, and instruments built by the firm were soon even better than the ones built by Orville himself. One such improvement occurred in 1908 when Lewis Williams, one of the five initial investors, came up with the idea of elevating the pickguard which was until then glued onto the soundboard. This change was inspired by the need—a constant one throughout the history of the guitar—to leave the soundboard as free as possible to vibrate. Gibson executives also decided to accentuate the neck-to-body angle on both their guitars and mandolins. This served to heighten the bridge, which increased the pressure of the strings on the soundboard and, therefore, expanded the volume of the instrument.

L-1 (1912)

Like the vast majority of instruments built by the Gibson company between 1908 and 1920, this guitar had a body made of birch. Arch-top guitars built by Gibson in these years have only moderate appeal to contemporary musicians and cannot compete with instruments built by Gibson after the mid-1920s. The Gibson logo on the peghead had just appeared when this guitar was built. Its slanted position was intentional; when the guitar was held in playing position, the logo became easily readable.

Gibson Style O Artist (1919)

In Gibson's time, the guitar was often used to accompany mandolin orchestras. This inspired him to come up with a new model: the Style O Artist, which featured a scroll similar to that on the mandolins in his catalog. This guitar, which was the most expensive of the Gibson line for quite a while, was discontinued in 1923. Several elements, like the tuning pegs and the pickguard, are not original on this particular instrument.

Lloyd Loar

Acoustic Engineer of the Century

Eddie Lang

This jazz guitarist was extremely popular at this time for his dets with the violonist Joe Venuti. Lang was one of the first to use the guitars developed by Lloyd Loar. These guitars has an exceptionally wide range and volume; players could therefore be heard in rooms with poor acoustics.

After World War I, Gibson continued to maintain its leading position on the market—though not without difficulty, as the mandolin fad was fading fast. This trend led to a change in the company's name, from "Gibson Mandolin-Guitar Manufacturing Company" to simply "Gibson, Inc." The Gibson designers also introduced a significant number of innovations. Some of these, such as the adjustable bridge or the truss rod neck reinforcement, are still in use today.

Lloyd Loar was a musician and acoustic specialist who had been hired by the company in 1919. Paradoxically, it was while working on mandolins, whose popularity was decreasing, that he came up with the most radical innovations the Gibson company had known since the departure of Orville. Loar, a mandolin player himself, made it a point to follow the prime concept of Gibson's founder: that is, applying the methods of violin construction to guitars and mandolins. Loar was thus the first luthier to replace the traditional circular soundhole with f-holes similar to those on violins or cellos. He also increased the scale length of his instruments and further developed the idea of an elevated fingerboard that would no longer touch the soundboard (an idea which, as we discovered earlier, dates back to Stauffer and Lacôte).

But Loar's main secret, and still the most difficult to analyze today, is his concept of "harmonizing" the different components that make up an instrument. Loar believed that each individual piece of wood has its own specific nature, flexibility, and resonance. Therefore, he customized each soundboard, brace, and back, and adapted the size of every f-hole, such that each instrument was perfectly suited to the materials from which it was made. This process was long and arduous, and Loar graced each of the instruments he had supervised with a label bearing his signature.

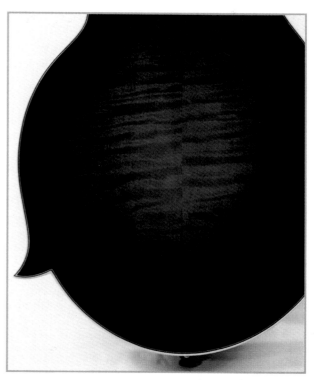

Lloyd Loar F-5 (1924)

The back of this instrument, like most made by Lloyd Loar, was carved out of two symmetrical pieces of book-matched curly maple. In this way, the luthier could create a stunning visual effect by using the mirror-like symmetry between the two halves, and at the same time balance the acoustical reaction of his instrument. This technique was obviously inspired by the work of old-world violin craftsmen, who had been using this principle for centuries. However, the types of wood used were different; the New-England maple used for this mandolin has acoustic qualities that differ from that of the European maple.

Lloyd Loar F-5 (1924)

This mandolin, signed March 31, 1924, by Lloyd Loar, is in remarkable original condition. The "fern" peghead motif is rare on Loar-signed instruments (only about ten of them were made), but is found on most mandolins made after his departure from Gibson in late 1924. Lloyd Loar's mandolins were a perfect success, aesthetically as well as acoustically, and are still the standard by which the quality of modern instruments are measured.

This innovative engineer also originated a series of instruments called the "Master Models," which included a line of mandolins (F-5); mandolas (H-5, which corresponds to the alto in the classical string quartet); mandocellos (K-5, related to the cello); and of course the L-5, which many consider to be the first jazz guitar.

Loar's tenure at Gibson was not very long, with disagreements over the purpose of his research finally resulting in an amicable parting. After leaving Gibson, he formed his own company, called Vivi-Tone, which was one of the first to manufacture electric guitars and violins. Loar, who was a pioneer in this field as well, had tried in vain to introduce his ideas about electrifying instruments during his time at Gibson. A few prototypes had even been created, but his concept, probably too far ahead of its time, did not meet with public acceptance.

Lloyd Loar F-5 (1924)

The upper part of the fingerboard does not rest on the top of the instrument; it is instead suspended over the soundboard without touching it. The soundboard, with a beautiful dark sunburst finish, is made of Adirondack spruce, a very resonant hardwood. This mandolin was originally equipped by Loar with a "Virzi-Tone Producer," a controversial appendage that was attached to the inside of the soundboard to improve the instrument's volume. It has since been removed from this particular mandolin.

Lloyd Loar

Between 1922 and 1924, Lloyd Loar (right) signed just over 200 mandolins and a few dozen guitars. Today, Loar-signed instruments are extremely sought-after and command impressive prices.

The L-5 and Super 400

The Birth of the Jazz Guitar

Lloyd Loar's innovations coincided with a period of great musical change in the United States. The 1920s, as we know, were a lighthearted, festive era in which music was celebrated and jazz reigned supreme. Bands were becoming larger and more sophisticated, but the banjo, commonly used in the Dixieland groups of New Orleans or Chicago, seemed unwilling to budge from center stage.

Although eager pioneers like Eddie Lang adopted the L-5 at its inception, the guitar still had a hard time finding its place, probably because of its limited volume. The banjo, despite its other limitations, could be heard over a large band that included drums and horns. The guitar could not match this feat. The first instruments launched by Lloyd Loar partially solved this problem, but it was not until the advent of the Big Bands in the 1930s, coupled with a few new guitar improvements launched by Gibson, that the banjo finally abdicated its reigning position on the bandstand.

Gibson was at that time fighting an expensive battle with its competitors—particularly with Epiphone who offered a wide selection of models for every taste and every budget. In the early 1930s, at the height of the Depression, the Gibson company, under the guidance of one of its greatest directors, Guy Hart, began to launch relatively inexpensive models such as the L-10, the L-12, and then the L-7. In 1934, the company enlarged all these models from 16 to 17 inches.

That same year, a new step was taken toward greater proportions and optimal volume: Gibson launched an 18-inch guitar, the Super 400, which today remains one of the most sought-after jazz models ever. This instrument was not only more resonant, it was superbly constructed with choice materials and exceptional ornamentation. Once more, Gibson was an industry trailblazer. Its competitors soon adjusted their own patterns to match Gibson's new standards. Some builders, like Stromberg, attempted to launch even larger instruments, but with the 18 inches of the Super 400, Gibson seemed to have found the ideal middle ground for both comfort and efficiency. First offered in a sunburst finish with a subtle gradation of color from brownish-red to yellow, the Super 400 was also available in a natural finish or with a cutaway starting in 1939.

In the ongoing effort to improve the guitar's volume, the final innovation of this time period (one that seems obvious today) was the use of electricity. Gibson, as we learned, did not initially put much stock in Lloyd Loar's early experiments with electric instruments. And, although the company did keep experimenting until the end of the 1920s based on the groundwork laid by the great engineer, it ultimately took the pressure of competition to convince Kalamazoo headquarters to launch their first electric instruments. Curiously, Gibson began by electrifying a

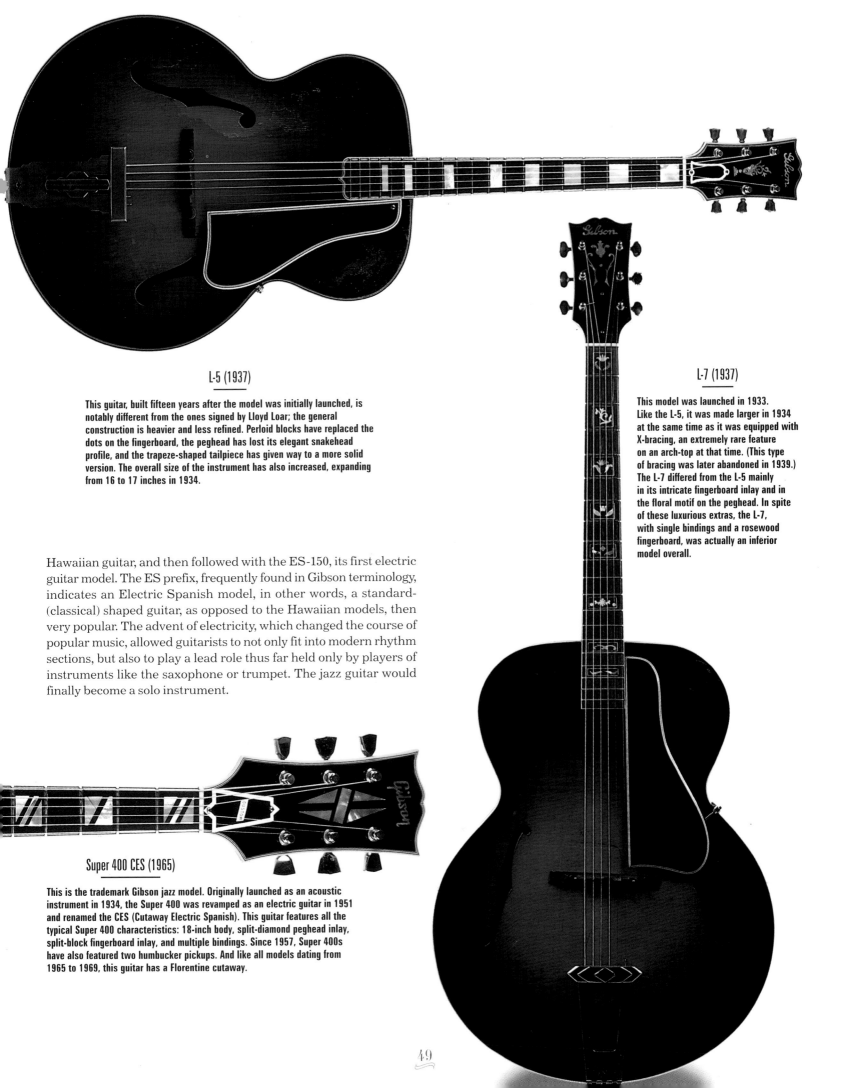

L-5 (1937)

This guitar, built fifteen years after the model was initially launched, is notably different from the ones signed by Lloyd Loar; the general construction is heavier and less refined. Perloid blocks have replaced the dots on the fingerboard, the peghead has lost its elegant snakehead profile, and the trapeze-shaped tailpiece has given way to a more solid version. The overall size of the instrument has also increased, expanding from 16 to 17 inches in 1934.

L-7 (1937)

This model was launched in 1933. Like the L-5, it was made larger in 1934 at the same time as it was equipped with X-bracing, an extremely rare feature on an arch-top at that time. (This type of bracing was later abandoned in 1939.) The L-7 differed from the L-5 mainly in its intricate fingerboard inlay and in the floral motif on the peghead. In spite of these luxurious extras, the L-7, with single bindings and a rosewood fingerboard, was actually an inferior model overall.

Hawaiian guitar, and then followed with the ES-150, its first electric guitar model. The ES prefix, frequently found in Gibson terminology, indicates an Electric Spanish model, in other words, a standard-(classical) shaped guitar, as opposed to the Hawaiian models, then very popular. The advent of electricity, which changed the course of popular music, allowed guitarists to not only fit into modern rhythm sections, but also to play a lead role thus far held only by players of instruments like the saxophone or trumpet. The jazz guitar would finally become a solo instrument.

Super 400 CES (1965)

This is the trademark Gibson jazz model. Originally launched as an acoustic instrument in 1934, the Super 400 was revamped as an electric guitar in 1951 and renamed the CES (Cutaway Electric Spanish). This guitar features all the typical Super 400 characteristics: 18-inch body, split-diamond peghead inlay, split-block fingerboard inlay, and multiple bindings. Since 1957, Super 400s have also featured two humbucker pickups. And like all models dating from 1965 to 1969, this guitar has a Florentine cutaway.

Gibson Jazz Guitars
The Advent of Electricity

L-5 CES (1965)

At the end of 1960, the L-5 CES (like the Super 400) featured a pointed Florentine cutaway. Its curved back was made of plywood, and was no longer carved from a single piece of wood. The guitar shown here has its original, very rare black finish.

L-5 CES (1978)

In the 1970s, Gibson returned to the rounded Venetian cutaway. Though considered more aesthetically appealing by many, this type of cutaway is not as convenient for treble access. (This can be seen clearly when compared to the 1965 model at left; the pickguards of both guitars are the same size.) The company also abandoned the plywood back and returned to a solid construction.

Wes Montgomery

This jazz guitarist, one of the greatest, became famous in the 1950s and 1960s for his solo recordings, as well as for his recordings with Lionel Hampton and John Coltrane. He developed a unique style of playing, strumming the strings with his thumb instead of with a pick like most jazz guitarists. His instrument of choice was most often an L-5 Gibson.

The ES-150, with its flat back and sparse ornamentation, did not look like an upscale guitar. Nevertheless, this guitar is still known and appreciated today as the model that introduced Gibson's first electromagnetic pickup. The principle of this now commonplace microphone is well known. Made out of a coil and magnet (or several magnets), it rests on the soundboard underneath the strings. When the strings start to vibrate in this magnetic field, they create a small electrical current which, once amplified, is converted into sound waves with the help of speakers. The first pickups built by Gibson, with their distinctive hexagonal shape, are now commonly referred to by the name of the first famous musician who used them : Charlie Christian. Gibson launched a few other models before the war: the ES-100, a cheaper version of the 150; the ES-250, which was, on the contrary, an upgrade; and the ES-300, whose slanted pickup did not last past the war.

World War II was a difficult time for most guitar makers: Gibson, like many of its competitors, had to interrupt the production of many models in 1942 to concentrate on the war effort.

When the company returned to full production, the musical world had changed tremendously, and the electric guitar had finally gained recognition as a legitimate and distinct instrument, one that made acoustic jazz guitars seem rather obsolete. Gibson began its revival in 1946 by reintroducing its most popular pre-war models, such as the ES-150 or ES-300. This time they were equipped with a new type of pickup, the P-90. On this device, the strings' vibrations were not picked up by a single rod connected to a magnet, but rather by six individual, adjustable contacts. An earlier version of a similar pickup had been briefly experimented with on the pre-war ES-150. In 1949, two new models appeared: the ES-5, featuring three pickups and a rounded, or Venetian, cutaway; and the ES-175, with a single P-90 and a pointed, or Florentine, cutaway. The latter model was particularly popular among jazz musicians. Finally, in 1951, Gibson launched electric versions of two of its legendary models: the L-5 and the Super 400, re-christened the L-5 CES and the Super 400 CES. These models found their way into the hands of musicians of very diverse backgrounds. Bill Haley and Scotty Moore, alongside Elvis, chose the Super 400 CES to produce their popular rockabilly sound, while country guitarist Merle Travis popularized his finger-picking style on the very same instrument. Even B. B. King was often seen with an ES-5. Gibson was truly becoming a universal label.

ES-175D (1961)

The original ES-175, launched in 1949 and featuring a single pickup, gave way in the 1960s to its sibling, the ES-175D, which was launched in 1953 and was equipped with two pickups. These pickups were originally P-90s, but Gibson eventually replaced them with humbuckers in early 1957. The 175 was one of the first Gibsons to feature these pickups which are now commonplace. This guitar, with its 16 1/4-inch body, is notably smaller than the L-5 or the Super 400.

ES-150 (1941)

The ES-150, launched in 1936, was the first electrified Gibson model and was immediately popularized by jazz guitarist Charlie Christian. This model is the second version of the guitar, made just before the war interrupted its production. Between 1940 and 1942, the model was equipped with a pickup that had a metal cover and adjustable poles, a unique characteristic in those days.

The Gibson Jazz Guitar
A Virtuoso's Model

Howard Roberts Custom (1976)

This model is somewhat of a step back in history, as it is probably one of the very few guitars since Lloyd Loar's creations to combine an arched top with an oval soundhole (rather than with the typical f-holes, which produce a more dynamic sound). This model underwent several changes following its initial launch, the guitar pictured here being one of its earliest incarnations. The fingerboard, made of rosewood on this guitar, would later be replaced by ebony, and the metal parts would change from chrome to gold-plate.

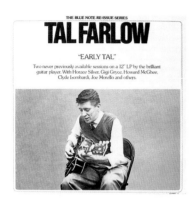

Tal Farlow (1996)

Tal Farlow was already considered a guitar virtuoso in jazz circles when Gibson contacted him to create a model with his name. He had always played an ES-350 (a full-sized model with a Venetian cutaway and one or two P-90s). Gibson, therefore, retained the body of this model and then enhanced it with a motif reminiscent of the scrolls on their turn-of-the-century mandolins. The guitar, which was also outfitted with two humbuckers, did not meet with much public acceptance. It was discontinued in 1967 but revived in the 1990s.

In the late 1950s, the jazz guitar, as developed by Gibson, began to lose a considerable share of the market to the solid-body electric guitar. Nonetheless, Gibson took a chance and decided to continue producing jazz instruments, and ended up creating a specialized niche with a loyal following. The company executives—remembering how their first electric jazz model capitalized immensely on its association with popular guitarist Charlie Christian—understood well that connections to a celebrity guitarist could do wonders for an instrument's sales and credibility. They therefore filled their catalogs with noted jazz guitarists, and the consumer could see such greats as George Barnes, Kenny Burrell, and Jimmy Raney vaunting the quality of Kalamazoo-made products. Gibson then went one step farther; it began associating famous musicians with the development and design of instruments which, once completed, would adopt their names.

One such example, the Byrdland, was created through the combined efforts of two Nashville studio musicians from the 1950s: Billy Byrd and Hank Garland. When a Gibson executive asked them to sketch the design of their dream guitar, they described something that looked basically like an L-5 with a considerably thinner body, shorter scale length, and smaller neck. This guitar, which predated the thinline models such as the ES-335 (see page 54), appeared in July 1955 and was immediately recognized as an exceptional instrument, perfectly suited to the acrobatic playing of be-bop and country musicians. (Hank Garland, in fact, was one of very few musicians equally talented in both these genres.) The Byrdland was a great success and, remarkably, still holds a place in the Gibson catalog today. Johnny Smith was one of the major influences of the cool-jazz movement of the 1950s. Smith, who was then using a Guild, was flattered when the Kalamazoo executives offered to launch his own guitar. He was equally pleased with the model Gibson designed according to his suggestions: an L-5 body, slightly smaller than usual, a Super-400 neck, and, most important, a floating pickup that allowed the soundboard to vibrate freely. In 1961, at the same time that the Johnny Smith was launched, the Barney Kessel model appeared, with its characteristic large peghead and unmistakable double Florentine cutaway. The Tal Farlow model came out the following year. Later, in the 1970s, Gibson approached Howard Roberts, an outstanding jazz guitarist and instructor at the renowned Guitar Institute of Technology, with a similar collaboration proposal. The company then reissued the Howard Roberts Custom, a model that had once enjoyed a brief yet successful run under the Epiphone trademark (which had since been acquired by Gibson).

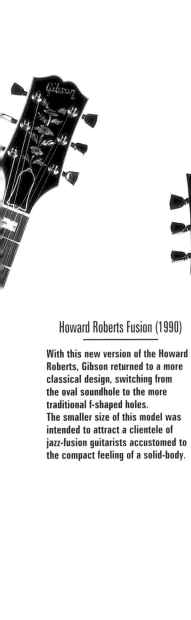

Howard Roberts Fusion (1990)

With this new version of the Howard Roberts, Gibson returned to a more classical design, switching from the oval soundhole to the more traditional f-shaped holes.
The smaller size of this model was intended to attract a clientele of jazz-fusion guitarists accustomed to the compact feeling of a solid-body.

Hank Garland

(Hank Garland was one of the greatest studio guitarists of the 1950s when he became the victim of a terrible car accident that left him half-paralyzed, abruptly ending his illustrious career. He collaborated on hundreds of recordings and released several superb solo albums, including the renowned *Jazz Winds from a New Direction*.

Byrdland (1960)

The Byrdland, released in 1955 and named for guitarists Billy Byrd and Hank Garland, was originally built with a Venetian cutaway. This particular model, launched in the late 1960s, was one of the first issued with a Florentine cutaway. Between 1960 and 1969, only 480 instruments were built with this type of cutaway—one that was much appreciated by musicians. The Byrdland is a rare model, particularly sought-after by musicians who appreciate its comfort.

Gibson Thinlines

Classicism Meets Modernity

In 1955, by launching the Byrdland and the ES-350T, Gibson had introduced the concept of a thinline guitar—that is, an instrument with an arched top and back in the jazz guitar tradition, but with a substantially narrower rim (1 3/4 rather than the usual 3 1/2 inches). These guitars, which also had a shorter scale length, were easier to handle and more comfortable to play than the traditional jazz instrument. Nevertheless, some solid-body players who might have been attracted by the velvety sound of these guitars and by their wonderfully playable necks, were still reluctant to adopt them because of their tendency to produce feedback. Feedback is a phenomenon well-known to guitar players who have handled hollow-body instruments. When the guitar is played at high volume, the sound waves emitted from the speakers bounce back to the guitar and are fed again into the microphone. This on-going cycle creates an intense, unpleasant screeching sound. Gibson found the answer to this problem in 1959 by launching a series of instruments that had the look and sound quality of jazz guitars, but were able to resist feedback as well as solid-body guitars. This type of instrument, called "semi-solid," was made with a thinline body whose air chamber was split in the middle by a solid piece of wood, which prevented feedback. The first and most noteworthy of these models was the ES-335TD, which was equipped with two rounded cutaways, a new feature at Gibson. This guitar, with a wonderful design and outstanding sound, was an immediate success and is still sought-after by musicians as well as collectors. Most prized are the models built between 1958 and 1962, with their "stud" tailpieces, (a cylindrical-shaped tailpiece hooked onto the soundboard, which is supposed to increase the sustain); their humbuckers with "PAF" (see pages 116-117); and with dot inlays adorning the fingerboard. The 335, because of its all-purpose design and maneuverability abilities, was soon adopted by many jazz-rock musicians such as Larry Carlton who played one for many years. It went through very few cosmetic changes throughout the years. Initially available in either a natural or sunburst finish, after 1959, the model was normally produced with the cherry finish associated with it today. In 1982, Gibson, taking note of the popularity of its own vintage models, decided to launch the ES-335 DOT, a reproduction of its early thinlines.

In 1959, Gibson introduced two new models which were upgraded versions of the 335, but which did not meet with similar commercial success: the ES-345TD and the ES-355TD. The 345 was equipped with two humbuckers, like the 335, but these microphones had separate outputs. They could be individually connected with a Y-shaped cord that allowed the guitar player to obtain a larger-than-life stereo sound by plugging his guitar into two different amplifiers. The Vari-tone, a circular selector of impressive size, let the musician control his mix. The 355 was even more elaborate, with a multiple-bound top, f-holes and peghead, and a Bigsby vibrato. It was usually equipped in stereo, like the 345, but was also available in a mono version.

In 1980, Gibson launched several models designed with B.B. King, the noted blues guitarist. The first two guitars, dubbed B.B King Standard and B.B. King Custom, both featured humbucker pickups and stereo output. The Standard, which was the less ornamented of the two, was discontinued in 1985, and the remaining model was renamed B.B. King Lucille in 1988.

Gibson ES-335 TD (1963)

The 335 is one of Gibson's classic models. Since its inception in 1958, its success has never waned, and it is an instrument especially appreciated by blues, jazz, and jazz-rock guitarists. The guitar pictured here, built in 1963, does not feature the PAF humbuckers of the early years (see page 116), and the dot inlays on the fingerboard have been replaced by rectangular block inlays. Originally available only in a natural or sunburst finish, the 335 has also been available in this characteristic cherry finish, since 1959.

B.B. King Lucille (1995)

Blues guitar player B.B. King came to fame playing a 355TDSV that he affectionately called Lucille. He once even risked his own life to retrieve Lucille from a burning club. Starting in 1980, Gibson launched several models bearing King's name, all of them equipped with stereo output like his original Lucille. Note that the f-holes on this guitar top are not real, but are rather trompe-l'œil paintings.

ES-355TDSV (1965)

The 355TD was generally fitted with a stereo circuit. The mix between the two pickups was commanded by the Vari-tone, a wide-diameter selector next to the Bigsby vibrato. Some models, however, were produced without this equipment.

ES-335TD (1965)

During the 1960s, these fingerboard inlays became rectangular blocks, and the stud tailpiece was replaced by an old-fashioned, trapeze-shaped one.

ES-335TD (1965)

Few details distinguish this 1965 model from the previous one, with the exception of the sunburst finish. This guitar is equipped with the famous vibrato made for Gibson by the Bigsby company of California.

ES-335TD (1967)

Gibson sometimes offered different options for the finish on its models. The ES-335 was generally offered in a sunburst, blonde, or cherry finish, but this specific model came out of the factory in a rare sparkle burgundy finish.

The Gibson Flat-top
The Referential Years

It was not until twenty-four years after its creation that the Gibson company finally dared to compete with Martin in the production of flat-top guitars. The company started by revamping one of its arch-top models, the L-1, simply converting its carved top to a flat one without renaming it. This simple mahogany guitar, small in size, was certainly not a luxurious model. Yet it did enjoy some fame in the hands of blues musician Robert Johnson. Two years later, Gibson launched the Nick Lucas, named after a very popular singer and guitar player of the day. This guitar, with its

dark finish and glittering inlay, seemed all dressed up for one of the brilliant parties of the roaring twenties. For several years, it remained the largest-bodied guitar of the Gibson catalog.

In fact, the Nick Lucas was a precursor to the "Signature" models which were guitars developed in collaboration with a celebrated artist who would later lend the instrument his name. This practice, which became more frequent in the 1950s (see pages 52-53), is now quite common.

During the Depression, Gibson started offering more economical versions of the L-1, namely, the L-0 and L-00, but never sacrificed the basic qualities of the instrument. These instruments most definitely offered good value.

With economic hardships lessening around 1933, Americans once again began to aspire to the finer things in life. Around this same time, Gibson capitalized on Chicago's Centennial celebrations, and on the crowds and media that this event attracted, to launch a new guitar. This model's visual appeal could not go unnoticed. The L-C Century had a fingerboard completely overlaid with perloid, an artificial mother-of-pearl then commonly used on banjos, and a body similar to that of an L-1.

It was not until 1934 that Gibson decided to increase the size of its models by introducing the Jumbo, a guitar of

Advanced Jumbo Prototype (ca. 1935)

This guitar, which is part of the impressive collection of Gary Burnette, is the Advanced Jumbo prototype, and was made in 1934 or 1935. Officially launched in 1936, only 271 units of the Advanced Jumbo were produced, and it was discontinued in 1940. When Gibson Montana reissued the guitar in 1990, this particular instrument was the model upon which the new series was based.

Gibson Tenor TG-0 (ca. 1930)

In the 1930s, Gibson, like all major manufacturers, offered guitars featuring necks identical to those on banjos. In this way, banjo players could obtain a guitar sound while still using their familiar chord positions. The tenor guitar presented a shorter scale neck and was equipped with four strings tuned like a tenor banjo.

Gibson L-C Century (1935)

Initially made for Chicago's Centennial exhibit in 1933, this highly decorated model was obviously intended to be an eye-catcher. The peghead and fingerboard are covered with a material called perloid, a synthetic mother-of-pearl. (The pickguard, made of the same material, is not original.) The fingerboard is decorated with rectangular blocks of rosewood, themselves inlaid with a genuine mother-of-pearl motif.

L-00 (1939)

This guitar made its debut in the Gibson catalog in 1932, but some units are known to have been built prior to this date. Originally produced in black, it was offered with a sunburst finish after 1933. This particular guitar displays a sunburst finish characteristic of the late 1930s, that is, one with a dominant clear color. The sunbursts on older models are notably darker.

similar size to the Martin Dreadnought, featuring a 14-fret neck. Despite its undisputed qualities, this model lasted in their catalog for only three years. Then, in 1936, Gibson launched the Advanced Jumbo, a Brazilian rosewood guitar, which was obviously intended to compete with the Martin D-28. The Advanced Jumbo, despite its amazing tonal quality that collectors are redis-covering today, was a commercial failure at the time. Only 271 units came out of the Kalamazoo plant, and production slowed down as early as 1939. It was then replaced by the J-55. Unlike Martin, Gibson did not have large supplies of rosewood. When World War II began and international communications became hazardous, the company was unable to maintain its connections with Brazil and was no longer able to import the precious wood. (Martin, on the other hand, did manage to produce D-28 guitars during the war and with only a few modifications.) These side effects of international politics probably deprived the Advanced Jumbo of the career it really deserved; given time, it might have given the D-28 a serious run for its money.

In 1936, Gibson also offered the J-35, a more modest and economical version of the Jumbo. The J-35 was particularly aimed at rural clients, who were substan-

Nick Lucas Special (1928)

When it came out in 1928, this guitar was the most expensive Gibson flat-top on the market, with a 125 dollar price tag, a fairly high sum in those days. The main characteristics of this instrument were its sides, larger than normal, and its slightly arched back and top. These details gave the guitar a deep, resonant sound.

tially affected by the economic recession, even years after the initial crash of 1929.

The war did not help Gibson's economic situation: a number of workers were drafted by Uncle Sam, and materials like wood and metal became scarce; guitars of this period reflect these restrictions. Nevertheless, Gibson did recover from these difficult years, and production began stepping up after D-Day. The J-45 replaced the J-35, a few minor details differentiating the two instruments. The J-45 was available exclusively with a sunburst finish (the J-50 was its natural-finish sibling) and, like other flat-tops made by Gibson until 1946, its peghead was adorned with a banner proclaiming: "Only a Gibson is good enough."

Gibson Southern Jumbo (1946)

This model was conceived in 1942 for Gibson's huge clientele of southern musicians, faithful players of the company's flat-tops. The Southern Jumbo was to take the place of the J-35 and the J-55 which would be discontinued the following year. The guitar pictured here, issued in 1942, was one of the first Gibsons without the noted peghead banner logo proclaiming: "Only a Gibson is good enough." At that time, the Epiphone company, which had not yet been acquired by Gibson, had replied to the slogan with an advertising campaign stating: "When good enough isn't good enough." Reluctantly, Gibson decided to remove the proud statement from its instruments.

J-45 (1953)

This round-shouldered, mahogany Dreadnought was launched in 1942 and quickly gained popularity thanks to the improved economic climate in the years following the war. This guitar features an upper-belly bridge, whose design was supposed to keep the soundboard from warping. The J-45, unlike the J-35, was only available in a sunburst finish. The J-50, launched in 1947, was actually a J-45 with natural finish.

J-35 (1939)

Launched in 1935, the J-35, with its mahogany body, was supposed to compete with the Martin D-18. After the Jumbo, it was the first Gibson flat-top model to possess the silhouette known today as "round-shouldered Dreadnought." "Round-shouldered" refers to its upper bout, which is more curved than that of a Martin Dreadnought. The guitar was initially offered only in a sunburst finish; this particular guitar was one of the first with a natural finish, which first became available in 1939.

The J-200

Guitar of Stars

It was in the 1930s that Gibson created the acoustic model that is still one of the most popular today and is certainly one of the most recognizable. With its rounded hips, floral motif, and mustache bridge, the J-200 (or SJ-200, as it was first called), is a unique guitar.

The 1930s saw a rise in popularity of the "singing cowboy." This hero of the black-and-white, Western B-movie experienced high adventures that generally included a predictable mix of wild rides, shotgun fights, and romance, all invariably interspersed with song. Since the ballads varied little from movie to movie, the crooning cowboys used fancy guitars to out-do their rivals. The best instruments of day were called upon: Gibson Jumbo, Martin D-45, D-28, and the like.

Then one day, the SJ-200 entered the scene. Ray Witley, a renowned singing cowboy, had been shooting movie after movie in Hollywood's RKO Studios when he met Guy Hart, one of the heads of the Gibson company. Witley described to Hart what he considered to be the ultimate cowboy guitar. Hart listened carefully to the actor's wishes and later invited him to Kalamazoo to supervise the creation of the prototype. A few weeks later the first SJ-200 was issued from the factory. Built of rosewood, the instrument was fitted with a unique type of bridge. Loosely based on those of baroque and romantic instruments, the bridge was long and curved like an Edwardian mustache. The instrument seemed to please Witley, and the SJ-200 was launched with high hopes in 1938. Interrupted by the war, it was reissued in 1948 with a few noteworthy modifications, the main one being a switch from rosewood to maple.

The model went through very few changes in subsequent years. In the 1960s, however, the elegant mustache bridge was replaced by a larger one. Shortly after, the dreadful "Tune-o-matic" was added; this individual intonation set-up system is perfectly suited to an electric instrument, but is rather useless on an acoustic one.

SJ-200 (1952)

Launched in 1937 and one of the most popular Gibson models ever, the SJ-200 was originally made of rosewood. Its production was temporarily interrupted during the war, and construction resumed in 1947. From that time on, it was made of maple and its name was officially changed to J-200, although some models, like this one, still bore the SJ-200 name until the early 1950s. The guitar shown here has been modified a great deal, and the bridge and pickguard are not original.

J-100 (1992)

Originally launched in 1939 as the SJ-100, the production of this instrument was halted when America entered the war in 1942. It resurfaced occasionally, and Gibson Montana finally reissued it in 1989. With its sunburst finish, rosewood fingerboard, dot inlays, and plain pickguard, it is an affordable Jumbo model, simply decorated with multiple bindings around the top.

J-200 (1996)

In 1993, Gibson Montana resumed the production of the J-200, using New England maple as on the models of the 1950s. (This wood had been replaced by European maple, a softer and, according to Gibson, less resonant wood.) Guitars like this one are also available with scalloped braces, and the more attractive mustache bridge has also made a comeback.

Bob Dylan

This popular folk singer, who always favored paradox and provocation, was often seen playing a J-200 in the 1960s. This ornate and showy model, then more associated with country music stars, did not impress many of his early fans.

The Sixties
Acoustic Rhythm Guitars

In the 1960s, Gibson made the most of the current music trends by releasing new models of guitars. The Everly Brothers, Don and Phil, were among the performers whose tunes rocked the daily life of every American teenager of that period. Born into a family of musicians (their father was a renowned finger-picker and a noted Gibson supporter), they had played instruments from the famed maker since their childhood, in particular two J-200s which complemented their elaborate duet vocals. So when Gibson contacted them to launch an Everly model, the J-200 was the obvious instrument to work from. Don came up with a double pickguard of his own; it covered most of the top and was symmetrically displayed on both sides of the soundhole. Gibson, however, was concerned that the J-200, still their bestseller, might suffer from the release of a such a similar new model. Instead, they decided to revive the J-185,

which had a Jumbo-like shape but was smaller than the J-200. In 1962, the first Everly models appeared on the market. They featured a standard spruce soundboard, maple body, stunning black finish, star-shaped fingerboard inlay, and the now-famous enlarged faux-tortoise-shell pickguards. The Everly brothers played an important role in the success of this model whose production was, nevertheless, discontinued in 1971. The Gibson Everly is probably one of the few guitars to have its own fan club. Based in the Netherlands, the organization includes famous members like British country ace Albert Lee, a long-time Everly aficionado.

(He actually owns one of the two original prototypes, a gift from Don Everly himself.)
The Hummingbird is another legendary guitar. Launched in 1962, it was one of the first Gibsons to deviate from the round-shouldered pattern thus far associated with the company's acoustic models. For the Hummingbird, Gibson designed a shape that closely resembled the square-shouldered Dreadnought, generally associated with

Martins. It was produced with a sitka spruce top, a mahogany body, and a smaller-sized soundhole, which increased the bass of the instrument. The finishing touch was a celluloid pickguard, lavishly decorated with a jungle-like fern and floral motif surrounding a hummingbird, hence the name. Young musicians immediately adopted this model, so perfectly suited to accompanying vocals. With the folk revival in full swing, Gibson's strategy was paying off.
The Dove, launched in 1962, had similar ambitions, but it was built of maple and its slightly longer scale length made it comparable to a J-200. The model also featured a Tune-o-matic bridge. This controversial metal system, along with the maple body, gave the Dove a unique sound—one that has both dedicated fans and steadfast detractors.

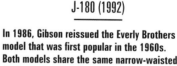

J-180 (1992)

In 1986, Gibson reissued the Everly Brothers model that was first popular in the 1960s. Both models share the same narrow-waisted Jumbo body, uniquely shaped double pickguard (a Don Everly concept), and star-shaped inlay on the fingerboard and peghead. The bridge on the new model, however, differs from the original. Note that the guitar pictured here has a custom, rather than the usual black, finish.

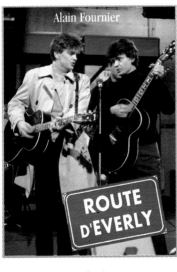

Alain Fournier

ROUTE D'EVERLY

Everly Brothers

This famous duo was rarely seen on stage or in the studio without their twin Gibsons. Gibson designers collaborated with them to create the popular model.

Dove (1960 Reissue)

Since its inception in 1962, Dove has remained one of Gibson's most popular acoustic models. The same original features can be found on the newer models made in Bozeman: the maple back and sides finished in an unusual bright cherry color, the uniquely shaped bridge with two mother-of-pearl inlays, the double-parallelogram fingerboard inlay, and last but not least, the highly decorated pickguard featuring the dove which gives the model its name.

Hummingbird (1970s)

The Hummingbird, along with the Dove, is one of the few Gibson square-shouldered Jumbos, and it was the first such model at the time of its launch in 1960. The design appeared during the peak of the folk revival when Gibson was trying to develop the ideal guitar to complement vocals, one with limited volume and good balance. Originally produced in a sunburst finish, natural finishes like this one became available only after 1963. The rectangular fingerboard inlays indicate that this particular instrument was built after 1973.

Gibson Montana

The Quality of Yesteryear

From the company's early days through to 1989, all of Gibson's acoustic instruments were made in Kalamazoo or in the Nashville factory, which was opened in 1974. As we have seen, the guitars built at this

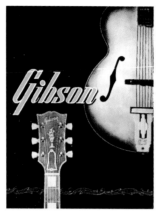

Gibson Catalogue (1956)

second site did not live up to the Gibson standard of excellence set in the 1930s. To rectify this problem, the company was in need of a serious overhaul and required an energetic coach to lead the way. Henri Juszkiewicz turned out to be their answer. Soon after acquiring the company in 1985, the new president set his mind on reviving the spirit of the company's glory days.

The Nashville site, which suffered from dampness and, therefore, hindered proper wood storage, was replaced by a new location in Bozeman, Montana, close to Yellowstone National Park. Under the spirited guidance of Ren Ferguson, an exceptional luthier who supervised the setup of the factory, and Larry English, the head of this new plant, Gibson gradually regained the trust of both musicians and dealers. As a matter of fact, its success was such that many experts predict that the acoustic guitars built in Montana in the 1990s will be equal, if not surpass, the quality of the legendary models of the 1930s and 1940s.

One of the first tasks of the Bozeman directors was to re-release the vintage Gibson models in formats that matched the originals as much as possible. Too often, reissues tend to focus on the visual aspect of an instrument without recapturing the essence of the internal construction and the acoustic qualities. In an exceptional departure from the norm, the Montana people, with a positive and open attitude, listened carefully to the comments and suggestions of musicians, collectors, and dealers. More often than not, the feedback from these groups was largely ignored by manufacturers. Gary Burnette, a musician and collector from North Carolina, was specially consulted when the decision was made to reproduce legendary models such as the Advanced Jumbo (see pages 56 and 57). Burnette lent Gibson the prototype of the model he owns, and his suggestions were taken into account. As a result, in 1990, Gibson started producing remarkable replicas of these all-too-rare instruments— fewer than 300 were produced between 1936 and 1940. In a similar fashion, the

Gibson Montana Custom Advanced Jumbo (1990)

When the Gibson people decided to revive the Advanced Jumbo model in 1990, they contacted collector Gary Burnette who lent them the prototype of the model, seen on page 56. The new guitar is almost identical to the original, but, unfortunately, because of the scarcity of certain woods, most units were made with a sitka soundboard instead of with Adirondack spruce. For the same reason, the body was mostly built with Indian rosewood. All the same, the Gibson Custom Shop does occasionally produce a few models like this one, made from the company's small reserves of superb Brazilian rosewood.

Southern Jumbo Montana (1990s)

Starting in 1991, Gibson Montana offered reissues of the 1942 Southern Jumbo complete with all its original characteristics, including the famous banner logo, "Only a Gibson is good enough." These perfect copies (compare with the model on page 58) are superb instruments, with a seventh-ply binding around the top, and a sitka soundboard adorned with a brownish "Cremona" sunburst.

Nick Lucas Bozeman (1990s)

When Gibson revived the Nick Lucas in 1991, they decided to feature its late-1930s characteristics rather than its earlier ones. The guitar is therefore constructed with maple instead of rosewood, and it is equipped with a 14-fret neck rather than a 12-fret one (visible on the original model on page 56). The scale was also slightly lengthened. As on the original model, the reissue has scalloped braces. The Nick Lucas is now available by special order only.

Nick Lucas and L-C Century were revived, as were, of course, such unforgettable models as the J-200, J-45, and the Dove. Gibson Montana, however, was not satisfied with simply recreating the past, as brilliant as it was. Luthiers and workers were asked to lend their ideas and skills to the conception of new models, some of which are now very successful: the J-200 Junior, which duplicates most of the characteristics of the J-200 in a smaller-size body; the J-2000, conceived by Ren Ferguson, which features a Venetian cutaway and a mahogany body similar in size to the J-185; the J-60, apparently another attempt at emulating the Martin D-28; and a series of electro-acoustic instruments called EAS.

Washburn

Mass Produced, Hand Finished

Washburn 355 (1899)

Consumers at the end of the nineteenth century were fond of any kind of elaborate ornamentation, and Washburn was one of the first companies to provide its clients with the highly decorated instruments they were craving. The ebony fingerboard on this guitar is artfully embellished with a mother-of-pearl tree of life.

The Martin company had always dominated the American-made, flat-top guitar market, mainly in terms of quality. Gibson, however, often challenged their supremacy in this field. But the history of flat-top guitars cannot be limited to these two makers. Starting in the late nineteenth century, many guitar manufacturers produced models that rivaled Martins, both in terms of craftsmanship and quality of materials. As for ornamentation or notoriety, they sometimes even surpassed Martin. The most important of these makers was Lyon & Healy. Founded in 1864, the company was named after its two initial associates, Patrick Joseph Healy and George Washburn Lyon. It started out by distributing instruments built by Olivier Ditson (see pages 36 and 37). Lyon next originated a line of instruments called Washburn which, thanks to very aggressive marketing, industrial-like labor planning, and a wide selection of models, sold extremely well throughout the country. It was so successful, in fact, that it is much easier to find a vintage nineteenth-century Washburn today than a Martin from the same era. Lyon & Healy was also the first to favor mahogany over rosewood for their guitars and to make instruments with considerably narrower rims. (It was not until the Gibson thinline models were launched in the late 1950s that a similar characteristic would appear again on any manufacturer's guitar.) Lyon & Healy also started the fad of decorating instruments with lavish mother-of-pearl motifs, a trend that prompted Martin to launch its forty-five models at the turn of the century. Starting in 1928, Washburn saw a succession of owners come and go, faced several serious bankruptcies, and even disappeared briefly after World War II. It finally re-emerged in 1962, and under the management of Roland (a brand better known for its keyboards and amplifiers) started producing new lines of instruments manufactured in Asia. Today's Washburns are once again American-made. Many other manufacturers were successfully building flat-top acoustic guitars in those days: Biehl in Iowa, Waldo, and especially the Larson brothers, who made some remarkable instruments that have recently been rediscovered by guitar enthusiasts. Based in Chicago, Carl and August Larson often crafted instruments for other makers like Stahl, Euphonon, Prairie

State, and Dyer; these guitars rarely bore the Larson name but shared common features and great craftsmanship.

The Larson brothers, originally from Sweden, built over 10,000 guitars, some of them with surprising innovations. They were the first to make instruments with braces strong enough to withstand the added pressure of steel strings. They invented a plywood-type brace made of ebony sandwiched between two pieces of spruce, which considerably reinforced the overall structure of the guitar. Unfortunately, Larson guitars disappeared together with their founders in the mid-1940s.

Washburn (1899)

The shape of American-made instruments of this period was still reminiscent of classical guitars then being built in the Old World. It was not until the beginning of the twentieth century, with the advent of steel strings and the quest for bigger models, that American guitars clearly distinguished themselves from European ones.

The New Guard

Heirs to a Great American Tradition

Since the beginning of the 1960s, the acoustic guitar has experienced cycles of popularity that have always been connected to the musical fads of the day. The folk revival of the 1960s, the advent of folk-rock, and the more recent "unplugged" movement have all created new markets of potential buyers. Consequently, new manufacturers are trying to challenge the supremacy of Martin and Gibson. Many of these new makers, such as Taylor, have equipped most of their models with piezo-electric pickups.

The concept of piezo-electric amplification, well-suited to acoustic instruments, was the first real alternative to the electro-magnetic pickups found on most electric guitars. The principle is simple: it is based on the ability of a specific crystal to convert mechanic energy into electric energy. The transducer, which integrates this crystal, is placed under the guitar's nut and transforms the string vibrations into an electric signal which is ultimately amplified. This system reproduces acoustic sound much better than the electro-magnetic pickups used so far. Contemporary guitar makers remain divided into two factions: the pragmatists, who see piezo as a good way to bring acoustic instruments to musical stages worldwide, and the purists, like Santa Cruz in California or Collings in Texas, who focus solely on the acoustic qualities of their excellent guitars and accept the financial realities that their high standards dictate.

France also has a tradition of excellent luthiers, and many guitars built there today are on a par with their American counterparts. French guitar makers—Franck Cheval and Alain Queguiner, for example—were certainly inspired by their American predecessors. Queguiner even did his apprenticeship with noted luthier Bozo Podunavac (see page 136), before starting to build his own high-quality models in his Paris workshop. Other makers with a more classical background—like Pierre Lajugee or Philippe Moneret, both graduates of the renowned school of lutherie at Mirecourt—also build first-rate flat-top guitars.

Larrivée C-10 (1990s)

Canadian maker Larrivée is known for his comfortable and beautifully decorated instruments. His inlays, especially those on his pegheads, are quite spectacular.

Gallagher Doc Watson (1990s)

For over twenty years, the claim to fame of the Gallagher family business has been creating instruments for legendary flat-picker Doc Watson. Some of the models by this maker are equipped with an ebony armrest that prevents the player's forearm from resting directly on the soundboard.

Taylor Gerry Buckley 614 GB (1995)

This company, based in El Cajon, California, and founded by Bob Taylor and Kurt Listug, produces a great variety of guitars with wonderfully comfortable necks. This model, the Gerry Buckley, is part of the 600 series, which consists exclusively of maple-made guitars. (The wood comes from the Northwestern coast.) Notice the Taylor bridge with its distinctive shape.

Franck Cheval Orville model (1995)

Cheval combines a respect for the legendary Martin and Gibson models with his own definitely French accent. The mixture of influences is particularly evident on this model which, although inspired by its predecessors, has a personality all its own.

Santa Cruz Vintage Artist (1995)

Based in California, the Santa Cruz company makes guitars with the same features as the acclaimed pre-war Martins. Their most famous client is jazz and bluegrass flat-picker Tony Rice (who owns the legendary 1934 Martin D-28 that once belonged to the Byrds' guitar player, Clarence White). Santa Cruz borrowed many features from the D-28, such as the extra-long fingerboard and the enlarged soundhole.

Alain Queguiner Jumbo model (1996)

The work of Queguiner, one of an ever-growing number of French luthiers building flat-top guitars, compares with some of the best American makers. This maple guitar with extra-wide rims was built for French singer Renaud, and has an exceptional sound.

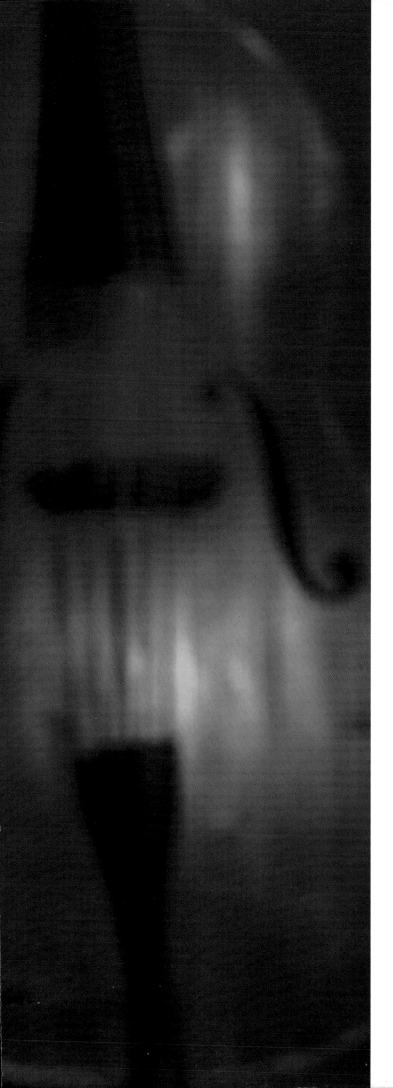

Other
～ Jazz Guitar ～
Builders

The Gibson company played a vital role in the initial development of jazz guitars, but it did not remain the sole producer of such instruments for long. Very soon, other companies acquired the know-how, skills, and materials required to create these instruments. For some, like Epiphone, their efforts would translate into great success and they would compete with Gibson on a similar level. For others, like Martin, the foray into jazz guitar construction would be a failure. Martin was encouraged after this experiment to focus its attention more exclusively on its long-time specialty: the construction of flat-top guitars. Arched-top jazz guitars were not only the products of major manufacturers; they also came to life thanks to the plane and chisel of independent craftsmen who built reputations for themselves through years of hard work and dedication. After all, it might be argued that the construction of a jazz guitar, in many ways similar to that of a violin or a cello, might actually be best accomplished through the solitary work and know-how of an old-fashioned luthier. In any case, it is certain that renowned guitar makers like Stromberg, D'Angelico, and D'Aquisto, as well as the many younger colleagues they inspired, contributed an important chapter to the history of jazz guitar.

Gibson wrote the book on jazz guitars. Capitalizing on the success of the genre in the 1930s and 1940s, many builders followed in Gibson's footsteps and offered similar models.

The Italian Connection

D'Angelico, D'Aquisto and Benedetto

In the early 1930s, many luthiers began to follow Gibson's lead and started building jazz guitars in the tradition established by Lloyd Loar. The first of them was a Boston-based craftsman named Elmer Stromberg. The son of a banjo builder, he started producing, in the 1930s, instruments somewhat similar to the ones of the Kalamazoo company. With their roughly shaped braces and plywood backs, they did not come near the same level of quality. It was not until the 1940s and the launch of the Deluxe—especially the Super 300 and Super 400—that Stromberg's reputation started to grow. The latter model (whose name clearly indicates that it was designed to compete with Gibson's Super 400) remains, at 19 inches, one of the biggest guitars ever built. Elmer Stromberg passed away in 1955, leaving behind 640 guitars.

Like Stromberg, John D'Angelico learned his trade in the family workshop, under the tutelage of his uncle who mostly produced violins and mandolins. Born in New York in 1905, D'Angelico opened his own shop as early as 1932 and started building guitars that were faithful copies of the Gibson L-5. In the late 1930s, however, he began to develop his own style and gradually moved away from the Gibson model—although he still wisely patterned the size evolution of his models after the ones of the Kalamazoo company. D'Angelico soon offered models with unprecedented characteristics; each one of his guitars had its own particularities. His most famous models were the Excel, with its 17-inch body, and the New Yorker which, at 18 inches, was in the same category as the Super 400. D'Angelico also came up with a number of aesthetic innovations, which made his instruments immediately recognizable. For example, his pegheads were adorned with a broken-scroll pediment in the center of which was placed a metal cupola, the whole resembling an amphora standing in an antique frame. D'Angelico also introduced a characteristic stairstep tailpiece, which was cast for him by a nearby Manhattan company and which remains his trademark. In 1947, D'Angelico began producing models equipped with a cutaway; these guitars are highly prized today as they are both exceptionally crafted and highly playable. When D'Angelico died in 1964, he had completed 1,164 guitars, all of which are highly coveted by collectors today.

James D'Aquisto, born in Brooklyn in 1935, started working for D'Angelico when he was seventeen. When his mentor passed away, D'Aquisto continued building his most famous models, most notably the Excel and the New Yorker, while slowly trying out his own concepts over the years. He simplified the shape of D'Angelico's models, and traded the heavily adorned tailpiece for an ebony-made version of his own. He also started building his pickguards from ebony, and his guitars, with their S-shaped soundholes and limited ornamentation, are beautiful examples of grace and simplicity. He was one of the rare luthiers to enjoy in his lifetime the profits of both his labor and of the collectors' speculations. Nevertheless, the prices of D'Aquisto's guitars really only skyrocketed after his death in the early 1990s.

D'Angelico New Yorker (1963)

Gibson introduced the cutaway in 1939, but it was not until 1947 that D'Angelico adopted it. He probably feared the extra amount of work this notch implied, but also considered that the cutaway might affect the instrument's acoustics. (One must remember that the cutaway was not done until after the top and back had been carved.) This guitar has a floating DeArmond pickup, which does not affect the sound potential of the instrument, the volume knob being affixed on the elevated pickguard. The peghead with its distinctive skyscraper logo is typical of the New Yorker model. The stairstep tailpiece is one of the rare features (along with the tuners and the D'Angelico logo) that were not made in the luthier's workshop, but were instead delegated to local manufacturers.

D'Aquisto Fender (ca. 1975)

In the 1970s, D'Aquisto designed an arch-top model that was marketed and distributed by the Fender Company. This model, which had many characteristics in common with the New York luthier's own guitars, nevertheless differed in terms of the soundholes and the peghead shape. Most of the soundboards on these guitars were made of spruce.

D'Aquisto New Yorker (1987)

James D'Aquisto, who apprenticed with D'Angelico, slowly moved away from his mentor's building principles. This guitar, built toward the end of D'Aquisto's career, features his characteristic S-shaped soundholes, as well a tailpiece and pickguard made of ebony rather than the more commonly used metal or plastic.

Benedetto Cremona (ca. 1990)

Guitar maker Bob Benedetto, originally from Florida, is known for his violin, alto and solid-body guitars as well as for his arch-tops. Since the death of D'Angelico and D'Aquisto, he is considered one of the leaders in the arch-top construction field today. He still works in the old-fashioned way, producing only about forty instruments a year.

The French School

Reinhardt and Selmer

Since the 1920s, France has played an important role in the development of the jazz guitar and has shown a real passion for this musical genre. It was only natural, therefore, that the French school of lutherie decided to add jazz guitar construction to its repertoire. Paradoxically, the vast majority of jazz instruments built in France can actually be attributed to Italian immigrants, the most famous of them being Mario Maccaferri, who originated the renowned Selmer model popularized by Django Reinhardt. (Reinhardt and Maccaferri, as it happens, never actually met.) Later in life, this highly creative character migrated to the United States where he built a for-

tune first by manufacturing reeds, and then by making the plastic ukuleles that were extremely popular in the 1950s. He died in 1993.

The Selmer company was internationally known for its brass instruments when it decided to try its hand at guitar construction. Mario Maccaferri was hired by the company to supervise the first attempts in that direction. A factory was built from scratch in Mantes-la-Ville, outside of Paris, and Maccaferri oversaw the production of the first instruments that came out of the plant in 1932. He would eventually leave Selmer on bad terms due to a contractual disagreement in 1934.

The Selmer Company continued producing guitars after Maccaferri's departure, with a few notable changes. The main modification concerned the soundhole, which switched from a large D-shape to an attractive oval shape known as a petite bouche, or "little mouth." Selmer also abandoned a controversial Maccaferri innovation: the double soundbox, which did not seem to be very efficient. The company did, however, continue to employ many of the inventive

Guidon (1995)

François Guidon is a French luthier who has been building arch-top guitars in the great tradition of Gibson, D'Angelico, and D'Aquisto since 1986. Famous guitarists, like French jazz musician Marc Fosset, play his instruments.

Selmer harp Concert model

This guitar features the famous D-shaped soundhole, typical of Mario Maccaferri's models. The Italian builder had already built some harp-guitars before rejoining Selmer, but this particular guitar is one of the rare ones he produced in the Mantes-la-Ville factory under the company banner. It is equipped with extra bass strings. The designation "Modèle Concert" (Concert Model) implies a classical-type guitar, meant to be played with nylon strings.

Italian's concepts, such as the reinforced neck and the cutaway (which Maccaferri claims to have invented, but which he most likely inherited from his Italian master, Luigi Mozzani).

Selmer guitars profited immensely from the publicity brought to them by Django Reinhardt. This gypsy musician was undoubtedly one of the greatest guitar players of his time, and he inspired many careers all around the world. He is still popular today, and bands modeled after his "Quintette du Hot Club de France" are more numerous than ever today in the United States. This might explain why Selmer guitars are extremely coveted and rare.

As noted by Selmer expert François Charle, less than 1,000 Selmer guitars were built between 1932 and 1952 when production was interrupted. Only half of these were jazz guitars, the other half divided among classical, Hawaiian, tenor, and harp models. Fortunately, many luthiers picked up where Selmer left off. Many of these craftsmen were originally from Italy, like Maccaferri. In the 1940s, Di Mauro, Busatto, and Favino Père built guitars bearing a strong resemblance to Selmer instruments. The industry is thriving today in France thanks to talented such craftsmen as Favino *fils* and Maurice Dupont, who keep the tradition alive. François Guidon is another noted French luthier, though he has quite a different style. More directly inspired by the work of Gibson, D'Angelico, and D'Aquisto, Guidon builds excellent arch-top models for clients worldwide.

Django Reinhardt

It is difficult to imagine Django without a Selmer. In fact, when he embarked for his first American tour, he left his guitar behind, confident that he would find many American-made instruments to suit his needs. Disappointed in what he found, he had his Selmer delivered promptly.

Di Mauro Jazz model

Di Mauro, an Italian luthier based in Paris, was one of the first to make copies of Selmer models. This guitar is equipped with a D-shaped soundhole, typical of the early instruments built by Mario Maccaferri for Selmer. Some gypsy jazz guitarists prefer this type of soundhole over the oval one, finding it better suited to rhythm playing.

Favino (ca. 1970)

This guitar, built by Favino Père in the 1970s, is a perfect copy of the Selmer petite bouche popularized by Django Reinhardt. Note that it is a left-handed model, which explains why the cutaway is located opposite the usual side.

Epiphone

Gibson's Major Competitor

An addition to the relatively small production of independent builders, Gibson had to face increasingly intense competition from long-established companies, such as Epiphone, who successfully tried their hand at jazz guitar building starting in the early 1930s. Epiphone, a company founded at the beginning of the century by the Stathopoulo family, had originally made their name in banjos. In 1931, the company left no doubt as to its intentions in the guitar field, launching nine arch-top models that were well received by the public. Epiphone was always aware of the smallest Gibson innovation, and would shortly thereafter offer the public a similar product. This practice made them the only serious large-scale competitor of Gibson in the field of jazz guitars. When Gibson started collaborating with noted musicians and illustrating its catalogs

with pictures of its most renowned protégés, Epiphone immediately sought out any celebrities still available and secured their services. When Gibson enlarged their models, Epiphone quickly followed suit and, in doing so, initiated a "size race," with each manufacturer alternately creating models of larger and larger dimensions. When Gibson thought that they had created the last word in acoustic jazz guitars with the Super 400, Epiphone responded by launching the Emperor, a model still revered today. In fact, acoustic arch-top guitars produced by Epiphone before World War II are currently among the most sought-after models in the world. Epiphone managed to handle the changes brought about by the advent of electricity, which it adopted as early as 1937, and even survived many financial difficulties, which resulted in a succession of various owners. The final irony, however, is that

they ended up being bought by Gibson in 1957.

Before being acquired by Gibson and for a short time afterward, the electric Epiphone models were equipped with a special type of pickup, called a "New York" by collectors, that featured six slot-head adjustable poles. Some models from the 1960s, most notably the Casino, which was a facsimile of Gibson's 335, are still appreciated today, mainly because they were played by John Lennon.

Epiphone Sheraton (1963)

This model was launched in 1958, shortly after Gibson acquired Epiphone, and it was clearly inspired by the ES-335 of the Kalamazoo company. It has a similar thinline body, the same semi-solid-body construction, and the same double cutaway. The model shown features mini-humbuckers, but the early Sheratons (up until 1961) had "New York" pickups. Note the floral peghead inlay, an Epiphone trademark.

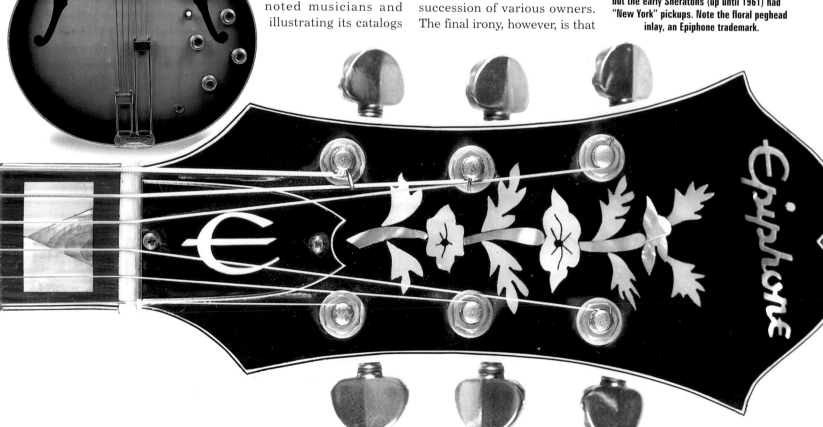

Epiphone Zenith (1944)

Also launched in 1931 as part of the Masterbilt series, the Zenith, with a walnut body, trapeze-shaped tailpiece, and unbound fingerboard, was a much less ornate model, and therefore much more affordable.

Epiphone Triumph (1943)

The Triumph was part of the Masterbilt series of arch-tops launched in 1931 by Epiphone to compete with the Gibson Master Models. It was a very popular guitar. This instrument, like all top-of-the-line Epiphones after 1939, was equipped with the famed Frequensator tailpiece, which created a longer string length on the bass side. "Frequensator" was short for "frequency compensator."

Heritage Johnny Smith (1990s)

Many makers offer beautifully constructed jazz guitars at a reasonable price. Such is the case with this model built by Heritage. It was named after the jazz guitar player Johnny Smith, who also had his own model under the Gibson label.

Epiphone Sorrento (1966)

Originally launched in 1960, this guitar, also a thinline model, features a single Florentine cutaway. It is also equipped with two mini-humbuckers, as well as with the famous Tune-o-matic bridge made by Gibson.

Dobro and National:
～ The Hawaiian ～
Tradition

The legend is good enough to wish it were true. One day Joseph Kekuku, a renowned nineteenth-century Hawaiian guitarist happened to drop one of the shell combs that held back his thick black hair. This accessory, as it slid along his instrument's strings, produced such a special sound that Kekuku put all his energy into trying to duplicate it, and thus gave birth to a whole new musical genre. He raised the strings of his guitar and used a metal bar to produce a whole new brand of music, one with a glissando perfectly suited the mellow, leisurely spirit of the islands. This new musical style remained for a long time within the boundaries of the archipelago, but, in the 1920s, a Hawaiian fad swept first the United States and then the rest of the world. Young women, especially, had a soft spot for the tanned island musicians with their unusual chrome instruments, and they convinced their boyfriends take up the ukulele or Hawaiian guitar. The fad was short-lived, but the instruments and techniques had a lasting impact. The Hawaiian guitar, for example, was the guinea pig for early experiments with electrified instruments, and it later evolved into the steel-guitar, an important instrument in country music. Today, thanks to the talent of such guitarists as Bob Brozman and Leon Redbone, Hawaiian music is enjoying a revival.

Hawaiian music, very popular in the 1920s, had an enormous influence on American popular music, from blues to country.

National
The Reign of Metal

In the 1920s, all guitar makers were trying to find a way to increase the volume of their instruments. One of the most important innovations in this pursuit was a metal resonator that enabled some guitars to achieve the volume of a banjo. Two companies played an important role in the development of these instruments: National and Dobro. Both companies were run at one time or other by the Dopyera brothers ("Dobro" being a contraction of these two words), and these two Czech innovators are generally credited with the invention of these resonators. How do these resonators work? The principle is simple: the guitar's bridge, instead of being attached to the soundboard, is connected to a metal cone that is vibrated by the strings, and whose function and form is not unlike a speaker. The very first guitars of this kind, launched by National in 1927, were actually equipped with three small resonators held in place and connected by a T-shaped bridge. (The instruments were, therefore, called "tri-cones.") These instruments were made of a metal alloy with a beautiful, chromed nickel finish that gave them an appealing futuristic look. The first tri-cones were offered in four different models, numbered Style 1 to Style 4 depending upon their level of decoration. Their distinctive chrome bodies were often engraved with intricate floral motifs.

National Style 1 (1929)

This model, which was issued in 1929, was the ideal instrument for playing Hawaiian music. The T-shaped bridge connects the three resonators which give the guitar its powerful volume. The model here features a square neck, designed especially for Hawaiian, slide-style playing in which the instrument is laid on the player's lap. (This also explains why the tuning gears are pointed upward.) Bob Brozman (above) specializes in Hawaiian music and is a renowned expert on National instruments.

John Hammond

This guitar player was one of the main forces behind the blues revival of the 1960s. Born to an affluent family, Hammond was one of the first musicians to introduce the blues to New England's art and academic circles. His father, John Hammond Sr., was one of the most influential music producers of the century, having played a role in the budding careers of such artists as Benny Goodman, Bob Dylan, and Bruce Springsteen, and even producing Stevie Ray Vaughan toward the end of his life.

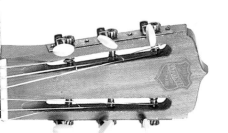

National Duolian (1937)

Perfectly suited to the blues, the Duolian, like the Triolian, is a highly prized guitar today. It was the first National guitar to feature a single resonator. It was intended to be a simple, popular instrument at the time of its release, which explains its lack of ornamentation: an unbound fingerboard and a plain, gray metal finish. The guitar pictured here has a non-slotted peghead and a 14-fret neck, two characteristics which appeared in 1935. It also has a square-shaped neck, a rare feature on this type of instrument.

Dobro

The Pioneer of the Resonator Guitar

Sheerhorn (1994)

Tim Sheerhorn is probably today's most respected independent resonator guitar maker. This particular guitar is equipped with both an electromagnetic pickup, visible between the two circular soundholes, and a piezo pickup. This combination, associated with a more classic microphone, offers the player an extremely wide range of sounds.

Since its creation in 1929, the Dobro company has distinguished itself from the National company by designing instruments with a resonator fitted into a wooden, rather than a metal, body. Aside from this resonator, Dobro's instruments were also equipped with two small circular holes, covered by wire mesh for improved sound diffusion. (The noted exception would be the aptly named Cyclops Model, which only has one such opening.)

This instrument was very soon adopted by country musicians, and became so popular that "dobro" is often used as a generic term to describe any kind of guitar with a wooden body and a single metal resonator. The Gibson company, which recently purchased Dobro, has gone to some lengths, including taking legal action, to ensure that this term is used exclusively in reference to instruments coming out of its factory. "Resonator guitar" is, therefore, considered the correct term for these instruments.

In the 1950s and 1960s, there was a revived interest in the resonator guitar thanks to musician Buck Graves, who often appeared on the highly popular TV show of bluegrass combo Lester Flatt & Earl Scruggs. Today, Jerry Douglas, one of the finest Nashville studio musicians, is considered the foremost specialist of the resonator guitar. Under his influence and that of some other talented musicians such as Mike Auldridge, an increasing number of guitarists are showing interest in this type of instrument.

It is important to note that since the war, the Dobro company has had many different owners, and the quality of its products has not always lived up to its reputation. This has given many musicians reason to turn to smaller builders like Tim Sheerhorn or R.Q. Jones, who both craft instruments of the highest quality. Today, however, under the Gibson banner, Dobro might just be on its way to recapturing the quality of its past.

R.Q. Jones (ca.1978)

R.Q. Jones was one of the first makers to offer wood-body resonator guitars that could compete, in terms of sound and quality, with the one built by the Gibson company. (Some experts believe that Jones' instrument is even better than the Gibson.) The resonator cover of this guitar, which was built in the 1970s, has been worn down by the impact of the metal fingerpicks musicians wear when playing this type of instrument.

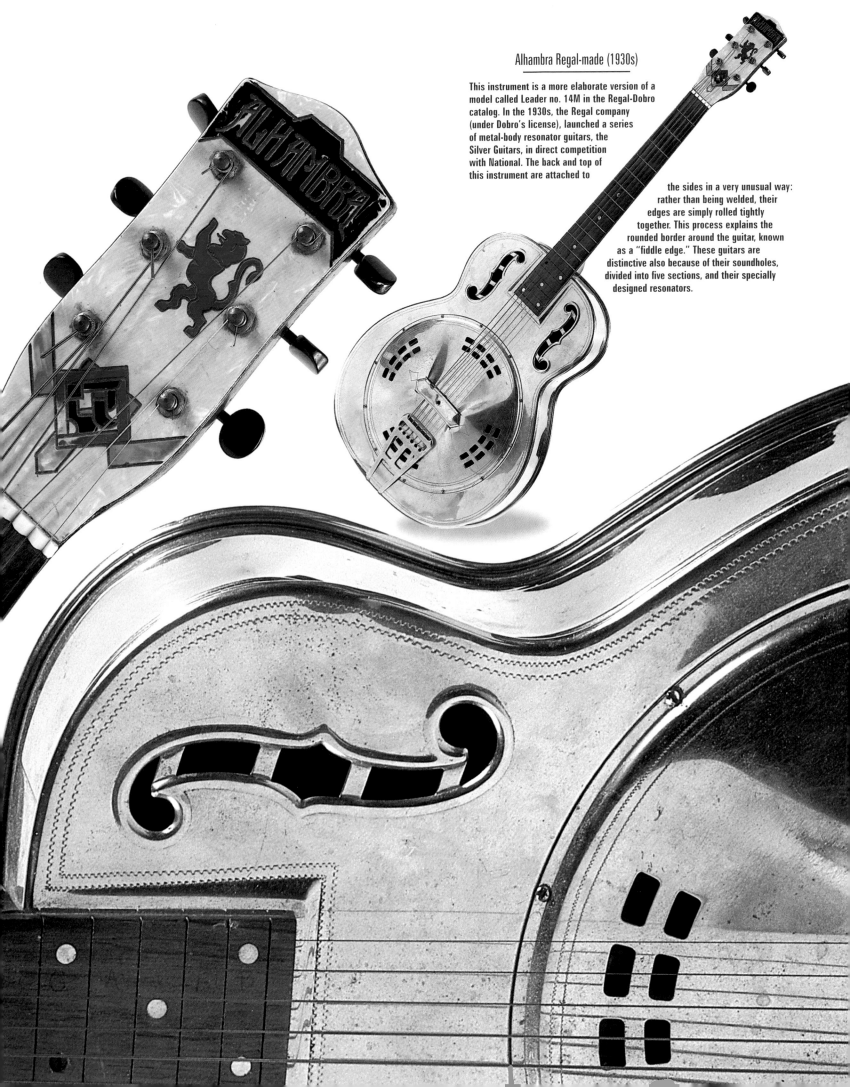

Alhambra Regal-made (1930s)

This instrument is a more elaborate version of a model called Leader no. 14M in the Regal-Dobro catalog. In the 1930s, the Regal company (under Dobro's license), launched a series of metal-body resonator guitars, the Silver Guitars, in direct competition with National. The back and top of this instrument are attached to the sides in a very unusual way: rather than being welded, their edges are simply rolled tightly together. This process explains the rounded border around the guitar, known as a "fiddle edge." These guitars are distinctive also because of their soundholes, divided into five sections, and their specially designed resonators.

Acoustic Hawaiians

The Comeback of a Century-Old Tradition

The Hawaiian music fad started in 1915. That year, a huge exhibition was organized in San Francisco to celebrate the completion of the Panama canal. The Hawaiian pavilion at this

event featured numerous traditional musicians from the South Pacific, and the American public was immediately charmed by their leisurely musical interpretations of the sandy beaches, sunshine, and palm trees of their native islands. The fad had begun; it would last until the end of the 1930s and would eventually spread around the entire planet. As early as 1916, a Los Angeles builder, Herman W. Weissenborn, inspired by the instruments constructed on the islands, designed a guitar made of koa, a Hawaiian wood with wonderful acoustic capacities. The early models launched by Weissenborn were immediately popular in the United States thanks to their unique structure. The neck was hollow and, therefore, the soundbox was lengthened with an extra chamber, which considerably altered the sound and volume of the instrument. Until his death in 1936, Weissenborn built many guitars, both under his name and also for companies like Konas, Hilos, and others.

Many guitar makers followed Weissenborn's lead. In the United States, Martin and Gibson, the latter with its noted Roy Smeck model, started offering Hawaiian models to satisfy the demands of an ever-growing clientele that was captivated by anything exotic. Abroad, several noted makers, such as Gelas and Selmer in France, also followed this trend. These Hawaiian guitars were often structurally similar to the standard instruments built by these companies, and usually differed only in that their nuts were elevated or their tables were reinforced to accommodate the metal strings. It is interesting to note that this same Hawaiian guitar opened the door to some of the most important acoustic guitar innovations of the first half of this century: increased size, reinforced braces to handle the pressure of higher-gauge strings, and the use of steel strings. Right after World War II, the popularity of Hawaiian guitars started to fade. Although it had a few brief comebacks—one in particular thanks to Elvis in the 1950s—for the most part, it became a forgotten trend. It was not until the 1980s and the efforts of musicians like Ry Cooder and David

Lindley that the acoustic Hawaiian guitar came back into the spotlight. In particular, these two musicians have repopularized Weissenborn's models, which they use in recording sessions as well as in movie soundtracks such as that of Paris, Texas.

Hawaiian Gelas
(ca. 1930)

This instrument is evidence that the Hawaiian fad reached as far as Europe in the 1930s. Many French manufacturers started building instruments for slide playing, and Gelas offered some very strange models. This guitar features a double soundboard; the surface on which the bridge is applied rests below a second surface which houses the soundhole. The nut is considerably larger than the fingerboard, and the treble string extends beyond the neck.

Ben Harper

Over the past twenty years, thanks to talented musicians like Ry Cooder and David Lindley, interest in the acoustic Hawaiian guitar has revived. Today, in the hands of guitarists like Jerry Douglas or singers like Ben Harper, the instrument is making a real comeback on the contemporary music scene.

Weissenborn Style 2 (ca. 1930)

This is the ultimate acoustic Hawaiian guitar. Instruments built by Herman Weissenborn between 1916 and 1936 are highly prized today, ever since their sound was popularized by Ry Cooder. The four models offered by Weissenborn all have a hollow necks lengthening the soundbox; this feature explains the odd shape of the guitar. This particular model, Style 2, was the second of the series and is easily recognized by the inlaid border around its soundhole. Like all the other models, it was built of koa.

The Lap-steel

The Hawaiian Guitar Turns Electric

When the time came to experiment with the electric amplification of musical instruments, the Hawaiian guitar seemed to be the logical guinea pig. This choice was made, in part, because it was the most popular instrument of the day. But it was also because electricity, which considerably altered the sound of jazz guitar and quite shocked the listeners of the day, seemed perfectly suited to Hawaiian-style guitar playing. Electricity magnified the sustain of slide playing, and marvelously complemented the playfulness of the style.

Many guitar makers almost simultaneously converted their instruments to electricity; their respective contributions are, therefore, difficult to distinguish from each other. George Beauchamp, one of the founders of the National company, developed an Hawaiian prototype equipped with an electromagnetic pickup, but could not manage to convince his partners of its merits. Disappointed, he offered his concept to Rickenbacker, who went on to launch the now-famous Frying Pan. This round-necked electric Hawaiian, with its distinctive "frying pan" shape, is today recognized as the world's first solid-body electric instrument, and therefore the ancestor of the modern electric guitar.

Ironically, National, which once discouraged Beauchamp from developing his electric experiments under its own roof, soon became Rickenbacker's major competitor. It converted to electricity in 1935 and launched a line of lap-steels, as well as lines of electric guitars and mandolins. The response of the larger manufacturers was rather delayed; Gibson, for example, cautiously awaited the sales results of its competitors' lap-steels before taking a chance on the new product themselves. In 1935, they launched their first model, and, in 1937, they developed a lap-steel equipped with a double neck. This feature offered the musician a much larger harmonic choice since the guitar could be open-tuned.

At the end of the 1940s, while Leo Fender was building his first models, the sales of lap-steels were beginning to reflect the decreasing popularity of Hawaiian music. However, country musicians had started picking up the instrument, and it would, in time, become a major feature of this genre. It was under the influence of country musicians that new innovations began to appear: for example, the instrument was set atop four legs and pedals were added in order to vary the pitch of one or more strings. This new instrument was called the pedal-steel guitar.

Rickenbacker Frying Pan (ca. 1955)

This model, first launched in 1932, is considered by many to be the first solid-body electric guitar (the neck was circular). Its production was discontinued in the mid-1950s, and this particular model was one of the last to come out of the factory.

Oahu Tonemaster (ca. 1930)

The lap-steel market was dominated by Rickenbacker, National, and Gibson, but many smaller guitar makers (which were often subsidiaries of the major ones) followed their lead and capitalized on the Hawaiian fad. This model, like all the others on this page, was designed to be played on the lap of a seated musician, with a steel bar in his left hand; thus, the name "lap-steel."

Gibson EH-150 (ca. 1937)

The first lap-steel produced by Gibson in the 1930s featured the famous "Charlie Christian" pickup, which had earlier achieved its notoriety on the ES-150. Despite of the decline of these instruments after 1950, Gibson kept making them until 1967. Most of the Gibson lap-steels were built of maple, enhanced by a beautiful sunburst finish. This model features six strings, but Gibson also built models with anywhere from seven to thirteen strings.

National Chicagoan (1948)

The guitar shown here is one of the very first made, since the model was only available between 1948 and 1950. With its spectacular oyster perloid finish and the musical design on its fingerboard, it is the ultimate kitsch instrument.

The Solid-Body

A Radical Change in Construction

Who invented the modern electric guitar? This is a tough question to answer. The idea of electrifying an instrument dates back as far as the end of the nineteenth century, and pioneers like Lloyd Loar had imagined the electric guitar as early as the 1920s.

It is important, however, to make a clear distinction between two types of electric guitars. The first type, which we have already largely covered, includes acoustic-style guitars, with real soundboxes to which one or more electromagnetic pickups are attached. This genre was popularized in the 1930s and was highly successful, despite its one major drawback: the presence of the soundbox, and therefore the potential for feedback, made the guitar impossible to play at a high volume. The second type of electric guitar, made from a solid block of wood (or later, from carbon fiber, aluminum, or plastic), is a completely different instrument since the pickups, rather than the body, are its most important elements. With this "solid-body" guitar, feedback is no longer an issue since the soundbox is completely omitted; the sole purpose of this instrument's body is to support the strings and pickups.

This second type of guitar didn't officially enter the scene until after Fender released its first models in the early 1950s. But the idea itself had been around for decades.

Consider, for instance, the famous Frying Pan launched by Rickenbacker in 1932 (see page 84). This instrument was de-

signed for Hawaiian playing, with the strings raised above the fingerboard. Unlike most Hawaiian guitars of the day, however, this instrument featured a semicircular neck, which would have made it suitable for standard playing if the strings had been lower. For this reason, many experts consider this model to be history's first solid-body electric guitar.

In the 1940s, many experiments were conducted, and the most celebrated among them came from the guitarist Les Paul. (His name became internationally famous a few years later when Gibson issued a model named after him that subsequently became one of history's most famous guitars.) The young musician, who obviously had a talent for tinkering with electronics—he was also the inventor of multitrack recording—had always tried to amplify his instruments. In the early 1940s, he built a prototype, now exhibited at the Nashville Country Music Hall of Fame, which experts nicknamed "The Log" because of is unusual design. To improve the sustain of his instruments, Les Paul attached the pickups, tailpiece, and knobs on a simple, rectangular piece of wood, the end of which he fitted with a neck borrowed from a Gibson. Then, purely for aesthetic reasons, he split an Epiphone archtop body into two halves and affixed them on either side of his basic "log." He presented his creation to the Gibson people, who didn't show the slightest bit of interest in it.

The company also rejected the creation of a certain O.W.

Appleton from Iowa, who, as early as 1941, designed a guitar which was remarkably similar to the Les Paul model Gibson would launch nearly ten years later—it had the same shape and arch-top. And, of course, no chapter on the history of solid-body guitars would be complete without mentioning the amazing Paul A. Bigsby, who later became famous for his vibratos, but who also built solid-body guitars for country music star Merle Travis as early as 1947. Had Bigsby possessed the aggressive nature and business savvy of a Leo Fender, he might have made solid-body guitar history.

Neither Bigsby nor any of his precursors had the determination nor the means to see their concepts materialize into something more than just ideas. It took the bold spirit of an opportunistic Californian, Leo Fender, to assemble all the pieces of the puzzle into one valid commercial venture that finally gave the solid-body guitar a chance at popular success.

The invention of the solid-body guitar was not only an important technical achievement; it marked the beginning a whole new musical era.

Fender:
～ The American ～
Dream

eo Fender didn't know a thing about music. At least that is how most of his collaborators affectionately remember him. The man who popularized the electric guitar and bass, and who invented some of the world's most successful instruments, might very well have been incapable of tuning one of his own creations. But just think of all that he did accomplish! Through his various models and his numerous inventions, Leo Fender had a direct influence on virtually every style of popular music in the second half of this century. From Jimi Hendrix to Eric Clapton, most important guitarists have played a Fender at one point or another in their careers. The man, though not musical, was very pragmatic, and his major strength was a wonderful combination of common sense, creative talent, dedicated professionalism, and an innate sense of design that allowed him to painfully give birth (the process was lengthy) to some of the most aesthetically appealing guitars of our time. Leo Fender, like Gibson, Martin, and Rickenbacker, lent his own name to his company. But, unlike these men, he not only gave direction, but also physically created from scratch the models that would make his company famous.

A Fender Telecaster and a Wurlitzer jukebox, two symbols of a carefree America in the 1950s that prefigured rock and roll.

Leo Fender

The Man Who Started a Revolution

Leo Fender was not destined for career in the music business. Originally from a modest Californian farming family, he was born in 1909 in Fullerton, near Los Angeles. Raised with a strong work ethic—he was later notorious for overworking his employees—he started out studying accounting and worked in that field between the two world wars. In his spare time, though, his hobbies centered around electricity and electronics. Like many of his peers in those days, he was an avid reader of do-it-yourself manuals and magazines, and began to build his first lamp radio-receiver and rudimentary speakers.

This pastime developed to such as extent that in 1939, after he lost his day job, he decided to open his own shop, the Fender Radio Service. He offered various services, from repairing old gramophone to the rental and set-up of audio equipment for meetings and so on. He also began fixing amplifiers and tinkering with microphones. Through various activities, he met several local musicians, among them Doc Kauffman, who played Hawaiian guitar. The two men formed a partnership, and starting in 1945, produced lap-steels and small amplifiers under the K & F brand name. But Kauffman, who worried about Fender's ambition and still had bitter memories of the Great Depression, decided to pull out the following year.

Not the least bit discouraged, Leo then started the Fender Electric Instrument Co. This company grew very rapidly, and in 1950, launched the first factory-made solid-body guitar. It was not an immediate success, but Leo was tireless and knew how to motivate his workers, sales people, and designers so that the model was finally accepted by the public. The Fender company grew as its products were steadily churned out of the factory, and it earned an excellent reputation in the 1950s and 1960s. In 1965, it was sold to corporate giant, CBS, for 13 million dollars, and Leo Fender stayed on as a consultant for a while. Unfortunately, the quality of the instruments steadily declined after his departure. (CBS would sell the brand twenty years later to a group of inside investors.)

Fender, of course, did not remain idle after quitting his directorial position. He created, most notably, Music Man, an excellent line of often underrated guitars and basses. He then formed G & L with George Fullerton, one of his associates from the early days at Fender. Leo Fender passed away on March 21, 1991.

Leo Fender

Ever the handyman, Leo Fender was happiest when experimenting on his new models and would not permit anyone else to bring his ideas to life. Not especially gifted at music, he nevertheless surrounded himself with competent collaborators who ensured that his concepts had a real musical foundation and purpose.

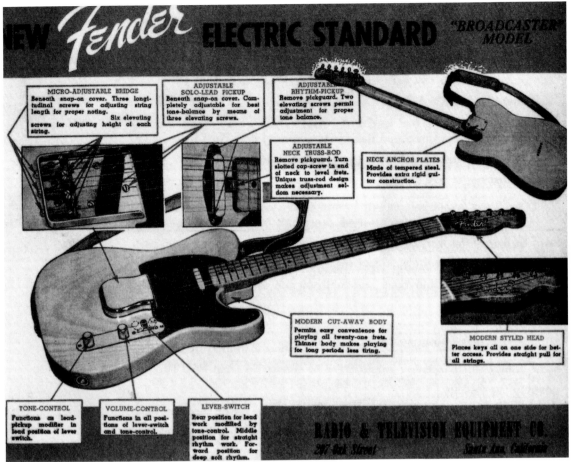

When it was launched in 1950, the Broadcaster (which a few months later became the Telecaster) was such an original concept that it threw the public off a little. Actually a kit guitar, it featured a neck attached to the body by way of four simple screws. In fact, each of its parts could be easily removed and changed, which explains why so few of these instruments have survived in their original state. The Broadcaster and the Telecaster differ in a few structural details; for example, below the Broadcaster's black Bakelite pickguard, there is no groove between the two pickups. Apart from such minor differences, the two instruments are practically identical.

This Fender Company advertisement is absolutely true: Leo Fender did start a revolution when he launched the solid-body guitar. His most important inventions—the Telecaster, the Stratocaster, and the electric bass—changed the course of contemporary popular music immeasurably.

The Telecaster

The Grandfather of Solid-Bodies

In 1950, Fender launched history's first mass-produced, electric solid-body guitar. First called the Broadcaster, it was renamed to appease Fender's competitor, the Gretsch company, which had already marketed a product with a similar name. At first, the part of the decal bearing the model name was simply clipped off. (The few such units issued without a model name on the peghead were later called "No-casters" by collectors.) It was ultimately named the Telecaster, and this denomination first appeared on its peghead in April of 1951.

The Telecaster was a very unusual guitar, and its appearance at first caused quite a stir, as the public of the day was unaccustomed to such a bold departure from traditional guitar-making principles. The most unflattering descriptions started spreading, with some people likening it to a canoe paddle, and others to a snow shovel. Evidently, guitar makers and journalists, used to the complex construction of jazz guitars and the elegant curves of flat-tops, were reluctant to accept this kit model with its body hurriedly cut from a piece of birch and its simple screwed-on neck. This approach was light years away from traditional lutherie. All the same, Leo Fender turned out to be right on the mark. The general public came around slowly, but was ultimately swayed by his minimalist vision, and this spartan instrument became a great success. Both elegant and practical, its every part could be easily replaced, and it could withstand the rough treatment regularly inflicted on it by the musicians of the day. It is no accident that the Telecaster was first embraced by country musicians. With its simple profile, conservative size, and twangy sound—not to mention its ability to double as a weapon in case of a barroom brawl—it became the preferred guitar of musicians on the honky-tonk circuit.

Leo Fender's methods of production, however, remained rudimentary. Although he excelled at inventing new concepts and keeping track of his accounts (his first trade), he soon proved to be a poor factory manager, unable to effectively run his workshops. Forrest White, a talented engineer hired in 1954, put the company back on track and saved it from bankruptcy. With one successful product and a competent directorial team, the Fender company was on its way to writing an important page in the history of popular music.

Telecaster (1954)

This is a beautiful example of an early 1950s Telecaster. Note the typical characteristics of the period: a pale orange finish called "butterscotch" and a black Bakelite pickguard. The chrome cover protecting the lead pickup was often removed by musicians who found it annoying, and few guitars of this vintage still have this part intact. Collectors often refer to this chrome cover as the "ashtray": a clue to the secondary use musicians gave it.

Keith Richard

This legendary guitar player for the Rolling Stones is often pictured with his old Telecaster with a humbucker pickup. Many famous musicians, from Bruce Springsteen to Steve Cropper, are devoted to "Tellies," as they've affectionately nicknamed them, and to Esquires.

Esquire (1954)

Although officially part of the Telecaster family, the Esquire differs from the Telecaster in that it has no rhythm pickup. Nevertheless, Fender used the identical body for both models; in fact, if the pickguard of the Esquire were to be removed, the cavity routed for the Telecaster rhythm pickup would be seen underneath. The Esquire's selector made available (until 1969) three different types of sound: a preset sound with filtered treble, a sound that could be modified with the tone control, and an invariable direct sound when the pickup was directly connected to the output jack. This last option, which gives the Esquire a higher output level, made it an instrument especially appreciated by musicians.

The Telecaster

A Guitar for all Seasons

James Burton

One of the most respected Telecaster masters, James Burton has played with many of the greats, from Elvis to Emmylou Harris. He is marvelously skilled at several special Telecaster-playing techniques, such as pedal-steel-style string bending and "chicken-picking."

Telecaster (1957)

Around this time, several changes appeared on the Telecaster: the original butterscotch finish was replaced by a more translucent, cream-colored tint, and the pickguard was changed to this white plastic version at the end of 1954

The Telecaster remained basically unchanged throughout the 1950s. Its most notable modification came at the end of 1954 when its black Bakelite pickguard was changed to a white plastic one. At this same time, the butterscotch finish it was famous for in its early days was replaced with a translucent, cream-colored one. Another change, less visible but very essential, concerned the pickups. The lead pickup (next to the bridge) on the early Telecaster had a wonderful sound quality.

A lot has been said and written about the construction of these legendary pickups, and some of today's experts, such as Seymour Duncan, are determined to discover Fender's secret. Everything has been measured: the wire's diameter, the resistance, the composition of the magnets. Other more obscure elements have been considered, some of them difficult to fathom, such as the effect of time on magnetism, or the number of revolutions on the coils, which could partly explain the difference between one pickup and another, since coils were wound semi-manually in those days. Duncan, along with other builders, now makes pickups that come close to duplicating the characteristics of the early Telecasters. These modern pickups, more consistent and reliable, and much better insulated, are a good option for the musician seeking a vintage sound. In 1954, Fender launched pickups with staggered poles. These new pickups had a harsher, more piercing tone, whose quality may be less appreciated by today's musicians. They are, nonetheless, undeniably exceptional.

Given the choice, many guitarists still prefer the sound of a vintage Telecaster over any other model. This goes for rock stars like Bruce Springsteen and Keith Richards, blues players like Albert Collins and Roy Buchanan (both, unfortunately, deceased), and even country music artists like Albert Lee and Vince Gill.

Fender Esquire Custom (1960)

The rosewood fingerboard, which first appeared on the Jazzmaster models in 1958, premiered on the Telecaster in 1959 starting with this Custom model. This guitar, easily recognized by its sunburst finish and white binding around the top, was the first Telecaster to feature a pickguard made from three layers of plastic in alternating colors, initially fastened with five screws, and later with eight.

Dating a Telecaster

The typeface and logo on the headstock are helpful clues when dating a Fender guitar. However, one must remember that changes in the logo decal appeared at different times on different models. As far as the Telecaster is concerned, its chronology can be basically summarized as follows:

1954

The guide between the E and B string has a circular shape. The company name is written in a fine, flowing script, which explains its nickname "the spaghetti logo," and the model name is displayed beneath it. The logo is located between the string guide and the nut. The tuning pegs are Klusons.

1966

From early 1966 to the autumn of 1967, the Fender logo evolved from its original "spaghetti" outline to a more modern one, featuring gold letters outlined in black. This is known as the "transition logo." Also note that the string guide is no longer circular, but instead has a butterfly shape, and that the logo now appears above it. The tuning pegs are still Klusons.

1968

This black logo with the gold outline is called the "CBS logo," as Fender had by this time been purchased by this company. The model's name appears in block letters beside the brand name. As on the 1966 model, two patent numbers appear below the logo. The tuning pegs are Fender hexagonal-shaped ones

1995

On many contemporary models, Fender has returned to a vintage look with its "spaghetti-style" logo. The logo is located below the guide, which has returned to its original circular shape. The perloid tuning pegs are Fenders. Note also the use of the rare quilted maple on this Custom Shop model.

The Telecaster
Variations and Adaptations

Fender soon realized that it would be a good idea to offer its products in many different versions; in this way each potential client would find one to fit his own particular taste and the maker could attract a wider following. Starting in 1954, the company made its guitars available in finishes other than the standard ones on the production models. The choices were at first, however, both limited and expensive. It wasn't until 1957 that Fender finally offered a real selection of custom colors that allowed the consumer to purchase an original-looking guitar at a reasonable price. In 1960, the choice of colors was expanded, and the buyer could then choose from among fourteen different shades offered in the catalog. These colors, made available to Fender by a company that usually supplied auto-makers, had poetic names like "Lake Placid Blue" or "Foam Green," that really had little to do with the shiny, garish tints they designated. It was again for aesthetic reasons that the Telecaster was sometimes decorated with an additional white binding around the top after 1959. Prototypes of this model were first made for the band of country singer Buck Owens. The resulting guitar, with a beautiful sunburst finish that accentuates the binding, was named the Telecaster Custom and has been a successful model for Fender ever since.

Telecaster (1966)

Although there are some rare exceptions from the early 1950s, it was not really until 1957 that Fender officially launched its custom-finish instruments. Previously available only in standard blonde or sunburst finishes, the custom-colored guitars from this period are highly prized today. This finish, called Candy Apple Red, was only available after 1960. The tuning pegs on this particular instrument are not original.

Telecaster Custom Blonde (1966)

Starting in 1965, Fender produced a few Telecaster Customs with a black binding (instead of a white one) around the top, and a white or blonde finish (instead of the standard sunburst). This guitar also has some standard features of a Telecaster from that period, such as the rosewood fingerboard.

Telecaster Thinline (1968)

Fender wanted to produce a lighter Telecaster and so came up with this Thinline model. The neck and pickups were the same as those on a standard Telecaster (although the pickups would become humbuckers after 1972). The main difference was in the body which was partly emptied out from the back to reduce the weight of the guitar by half. The instrument also features an enlarged pickguard and an f-hole on the bass bout.

Telecaster Deluxe (1974)

An odd hybrid instrument, the Telecaster Deluxe, launched in 1972, combined a Telecaster body (although the back was contoured like a Stratocaster to hug the musician's body), a Stratocaster tilt neck, and two humbucker-type pickups. With this model, Fender was obviously trying to compete with Gibson. The "tilt neck" on this instrument means that the truss rod bar is adjusted at the peghead.

Esquire Custom Shop (1990s)

Since its inception in 1987, the Fender Custom Shop's purpose has been to build, with the utmost attention to quality, limited series of instruments or unique models ordered by collectors or musicians. This superb Esquire has an emptied-out body, two bordered f-holes, and a neck made of spectacular quilted maple.

Albert Collins

Blues guitarist Albert Collins was a master of the Telecaster. He made wonderful use of the stinging sound of the instrument's lead pickup. Fender released an Albert Collins Signature model in the 1990s, which was patterned after the late-1950s Telecaster that the musician used during most of his career.

Telecaster 1969 with Bigsby vibrato

Starting in the early 1950s, some Telecasters were available with vibratos made by the Californian constructor Bigsby. This option, however, wasn't officially available until after 1967. Guitars that featured this vibrato had one bridge saddle for each string, instead of the three found on most Tellies.

The Stratocaster

History's Most Influential Guitar

When the Telecaster became popular in the early 1950s, Leo Fender, always anxious for feedback from working musicians, made the rounds of the local clubs and asked opinions of many artists. He wanted to improve the existing Telecaster and eventually launch an entirely remodeled one. Among these musicians was Bill Carson, a guitarist in many popular country-and-western groups, who evidently had a tremendous impact on the evolution of the instrument that Leo was developing, the Stratocaster. Among the most common requests made by Carson and other musicians was for the addition of a vibrato on Fender instruments. This system, already successfully developed by Bigsby, allowed the musician to lower the pitch of a note by activating a lever positioned next to his right hand. Once this lever was released, the guitar string returned to its original pitch without any interference. At least this was the theory; in practice, most of the vibratos of the day were rather faulty. So Fender worked on a solution. He designed a unit that combined the tailpiece, bridge, and vibrato, and attached it to the body with several springs that allowed the guitar to stay properly tuned. This new system turned out to be so effective that it remained the most up-to-date vibrato throughout the better part of three decades; the Floyd-Rose vibrato only replaced it in the 1980s. The musicians of the early fifties had more feedback for Fender: in their opinion, the Telecaster, with its rough, plain body and bland cream-colored finish, was not the most attractive instrument. Fender, therefore, designed a body that was partially contoured in certain spots so that it would comfortably hug the body of the player. He also decided to finish the new instrument in a two-tone sunburst, with color gradations from dark brown to yellow. With three single-coil pickups, a one-piece maple neck, and a bridge fitted with six individual saddles, the new instrument was launched in 1954 as the Stratocaster. It went on to become one of the greatest successes in guitar history.

Stratocaster (1955)

Launched in 1954, the Stratocaster was initially available only in a two-tone sunburst finish. The guitar pictured here is part of the impressive collection of Lars Henrickson, and is probably one of the very first ones issued in a natural or "blonde" finish. The knobs and pickup housing are not yet made of plastic, but still of Bakelite. The neck is solid maple, and the peghead has the typical, pre-CBS, Stratocaster profile.

Stratocaster (1957), Fender Super Amp (1957)

This attractive duo is of the same vintage. The Stratocaster still features the original two-tone sunburst finish (a third tone would appear the following year). The pickup housings and the knobs are made of white plastic. The Super Amp is equipped with two 10-inch Jensen speakers, and has 20 watts of power.

Fender Amp Princeton (1958)

Players and collectors are as fascinated by vintage Fender amps as they are by their guitars. Some of these amps, like the Bassman or the Twin Reverb, are especially valued by musicians who appreciate the warm sound of the tubes as well as the quality of the Jensen speakers. That having been said, this Princeton, with merely 4.5 watts of power, would have a hard time competing with any of today's models.

The Stratocaster

The Guitar of Rock Superstars

In 1959, Fender stopped using solid maple necks and instead equipped the Stratocaster, like all of its models, with a maple neck covered with a rosewood fingerboard. Up until 1962, this additional fingerboard had a slightly curved upper surface, but the part in contact with the neck was flat. This rather thick fingerboard was known as a "slab-board." In 1962, the lower surface of the fingerboard was made parallel to the upper one—both slightly curved—and it was then known as the "curved-board." These details, among many others, help experts accu-

rately date these instruments. But more importantly, this combination of maple and rosewood on the neck had a major impact on the sound of the instrument, with rosewood rounding out the sharper sound of maple. The unique sound quality of these instruments, combined with their superior craftsmanship compared to the post-CBS models, explains why Stratocasters from the early 1960s are so legendary. Equipped with a curved-board, these "L-Series" Stratocasters (as they are respectfully known among aficionados) are the models

most highly regarded by musicians, even if collectors generally prefer the 1950s models or the custom-colored ones.

In 1965, CBS took over the management and ownership of the Fender company, and the quality of the instruments gradually started to decline. Guitars from this period are easily identified by their enlarged pegheads, among other structural details. CBS kept producing instruments with the curved rosewood fingerboards,

but, after 1967, began to also offer instruments with maple necks and veneered maple fingerboards. These models, quite rare, were used by Jimi Hendrix with obviously successful results and are highly sought after today.

In 1971, Leo Fender, who was still employed as a consultant by the Fender company, developed a new neck-adjusting device. Up until that time, the neck was reinforced by way of a metal truss-rod that could be adjusted on the heel side

ANNIVERSARY

of the neck. This method had one major drawback: the neck had to be unscrewed and removed before any adjustments could be made. Leo Fender came up with a new system called a "tilt neck," in which adjustments could be made on the headstock side of the neck, making the whole process much simpler.

Lefty Stratocaster (1965)

Strangely enough, "lefty" Stratocasters are most often sought out by right-handed players. Jimi Hendrix, who was left-handed, actually used a standard right-handed instrument, and for this reason, the vibrato on his instrument would appear to be in reverse. This is why many right-handed players, wanting to emulate Hendrix's style, are fond of this type of instrument.

Stratocaster (1962)

A rare model in a blonde finish. The rosewood fingerboard was standard since 1959, but this particular guitar is one of the first to feature a "curved board" in which the underside of the board is curved in a parallel fashion to the upper surface. All Stratocasters were built of ash in the 1950s, but in the 1960s, Fender used this wood exclusively for blonde models such as this one. Other Stratocasters were eventually made of alder. Over time, the plastic pickguard of this model has taken on a greenish tint, typical of guitars of this era.

Stratocaster (1965)

In 1962, Fender launched a new serial number system for his instruments, with an L preceding a five-digit number. Instruments from this period are collected, but they are not rare by vintage standards; between 1962 and late 1965, 100,000 of them were built! This superb Lake Placid Blue model is one of the last of the series.

Stratocaster Anniversary (1970s)

Launched to celebrate the model's twenty-fifth birthday, this series featured several innovations such as a return to the old-style adjustable neck, marking the end of the "tilt neck" of the 1970s. The peghead still has the enlarged profile typical of that period.

The Stratocaster

Still Attractive in her Forties

Starting in 1981, the Fender company, under new direction, wisely looked to its own past and decided to reissue some older models like the Stratocaster 57 and 62; it also launched several new models that definitely looked to the future. Around that time, the company also started to resolve some of its financial difficulties by relocating part of its operations first to Japan, and then to South Korea, and by introducing a line of lower-priced instruments, called Squiers. These guitars made it possible for Fender to compete with Asian manufacturers whose products were helped by the rising U.S. dollar. Fender's first attempt at building a contemporary model was a failure: the Stratocaster Elite, with active electronics and a new type of vibrato (that turned out to be a disaster) came close to sinking the company which had already been experi-

encing serious difficulties. Fortunately, the company executives, most notably Dan Smith, next made some prudent decisions. A new plant was opened in Corona, a few miles away from the original one in Fullerton, and the American Standard model was launched. This guitar brilliantly combined the classic features of the original Stratocaster with some thoroughly modern touches, such as a more effective vibrato. The model was an enormous success, and allowed the company

to face the end of the century in much better financial health. In 1987, Fender produced the Strat Plus, which featured a new type of pickup called the Lace Sensor. Then, throughout the 1990s, the company launched various Signature models—as was done with the Telecaster— which were conceived by many guitar

greats. One of these was the Eric Clapton, which shares some characteristics with Blackie, the guitar player's favorite Stratocaster, as well as the neck profile of one of his old Martins. Next came the Yngwie

Malmsteen model with its scalloped fingerboard; the Stevie Ray Vaughan model with its reverse vibrato arm (a nod to Jimi Hendrix); the Robert Cray; and the reissue of the Mary Kaye, a model first launched in the 1950s dedicated a noted female guitarist of the day, which was in fact the precursor to the whole concept of Signature guitars.

Far from the expensive Custom Shop instruments is the Jimmy Vaughan model, launched by Fender at the end of 1997 and named for the brother of Stevie Ray and longtime leader of the Fabulous Thunderbirds. It was built in Mexico to keep production costs low, as it was Vaughan's wish that his model be an affordably priced one.

Mary Kaye Stratocaster 62 Reissue

In the 1950s, a guitar player named Mary Kaye appeared in the Fender catalogs to promote a Stratocaster with a translucent blonde finish and gold-plated metal parts. Originals of this guitar command very high prices today, but Fender reissued the model, with its original maple neck, between 1987 and 1989. This guitar shown here is somewhat unusual, as it is a Mary Kaye with a rosewood fingerboard.

Eric Clapton Stratocaster (1991)

The Eric Clapton model was the first Signature model issued by Fender, in 1988. This guitar combines the dark finish made famous on Blackie, the British guitarist's favorite Stratocaster, as well as an exact duplicate of its vibrato. When Fender made the pickups for this model, Clapton wanted the company to also try to duplicate the "compressed" sound of his old model. A compromise was found by outfitting this guitar with a Lace Sensor and active circuitry.

Lone Star Stratocaster (1997)

Targeting blues and blues-rock guitarists in particular, this model is known for its distinctive pickups: two Texas Specials and two Seymour Duncan "pearly gates." Notice Fender's return to a maple neck, an old-style peghead shape, and its vintage "spaghetti" logo.

American Standard Stratocaster (1993)

This model, with a rosewood fingerboard and three Lace Sensor pickups, is made entirely of aluminum. In 1993 and 1994, Fender produced a few models similar to this one, like the Harley-Davidson or the Freddy Tavares Aloha, but these instruments are fairly rare.

From the Beach Boys to Nirvana:
A Model for Everyone

In 1956, Fender augmented its line with two new models for beginners: the Musicmaster and the Duo-Sonic. These two guitars had a considerably reduced scale length and, therefore, less string tension, making them easier to play. In the catalogs of the era, Fender highlighted the advantages of these new models, pointing out that they were perfect for "beginners or adults with small hands." The Musicmaster and the Duo-Sonic, outfitted with one and two pickups, respectively, also had a reduced price: for half the cost of a Stratocaster, a beginner could acquire a simple but well-built guitar. Both models were a success, and their only weakness was the new type of pickguard they featured. Leo Fender, always the innovator, designed them himself. He came up with the idea of giving aluminum a gold finish through electrolysis. The effect was beautiful on a new instrument, but it wasn't durable enough to withstand years of use.

With the Jazzmaster, which first appeared in the catalog in 1958, Fender was simply presenting the "most beautiful electric guitar in America"; their goal was actually to upstage the Stratocaster itself. The innovations on this model were numerous: a surprising asymmetrical shape, a rosewood veneer fingerboard (the Jazzmaster was the first Fender with this type of fingerboard, which started appearing on other models the following year), a new type of floating vibrato, and, most important, a group of selectors that enabled the musician to play a number a preset sounds. This innovation was designed to simplify the job of stage guitarists, who had to switch quickly and frequently from lead to rhythm playing. Despite all these attributes, the Jazzmaster would not be a lasting success. Its qualities were most likely overshadowed by those of its two famous predecessors, although it did possess a few weak points, such as poor isolation and a tendency to catch every hum, making it hard to play on stage.

In 1964, Fender launched the Mustang, which was really nothing more than a Duo-Sonic upgraded by the addition of a vibrato. All these Fenders suffered from the popularity of the Stratocaster and the Telecaster, although some musicians did make good use of them. The "surfer" bands of the 1960s, as well as the "grunge rockers" of the 1990s, both contributed to the rediscovery of these otherwise forgotten guitars.

Musicmaster

Marketed as a student model after 1956, the Musicmaster originally had symmetrical hips, like the Stratocaster or Telecaster. Starting in 1964, however, it featured an off-body shape and was available in a white finish like this one. Its production was discontinued in 1982.

Duo-Sonic II (1966)

Launched at the same time as the Musicmaster, the Duo-Sonic was actually an identical guitar, except for the addition of two pickups. Beginning in 1964, it was available in a white, blue, or red (as pictured here) finish. The "II" indicates a guitar with a longer scale, available after 1965. The model was discontinued in 1969, when CBS drastically downsized its catalog.

Fender Mustang (1970s)

Very similar to the Duo-Sonic—they really only differ in that there is no vibrato arm on this model—the Mustang was available in a red, white, or blue finish. Its production ended in 1982.

Jazzmaster (1965)

This guitar's beautiful, rare Dakota red finish, which also adorns the peghead, is a unique feature of the Jazzmaster. When it came out in 1958, this was a very innovative model that featured a new type of pickup, a rosewood veneer fingerboard (it was the first such model), and a floating vibrato, without the usual springs anchoring the block to the back of the guitar.

The Rest of the Catalog
Guitars Seeking a Niche

Alongside its famous models, Fender often marketed guitars with unusual characteristics. These unconventional models didn't always find a niche in their day, but are now delighting vintage guitar collectors on limited budgets.

In 1962, Fender launched the Jaguar, an instrument that resembled the Jazzmaster in many ways: it had the same asymmetrical body and a similar separated bridge and vibrato (unlike the Strat). On the other hand, the Jaguar was outfitted with pickups whose base and sides were well isolated, to avoid the problems then associated with the Jazzmaster. It also featured a gadget that enabled the musician to mute the sound—an effect, in fact, that would be as easily produced by placing the palm of his hand on the strings. This system, similar to one invented by Gretsch, was really quite useless, and the feature was actually removed by most musicians. The Jaguar was a quality guitar and an upscale Fender, but, despite a good start, its sales quickly dropped off. In a similar way, the company also tried to revive the Musicmaster by creating a similar model, the Bronco, which featured a new type of vibrato.

A radically new concept emerged in 1966 when Fender launched the Coronado. Obviously the company wanted to compete with Gibson, which had had great success with its thinlines, particularly the 335. With the help of German designer Roger Rossmeisl, Fender produced a similar model, equipped with one or two pickups. The Coronado was, in fact, a strange hybrid, with a Gibson-like arch-top body and a typical detachable Fender neck, like that of a solid-body. The guitar was a failure and was discontinued in 1970. In similar attempts, Fender later launched other hollow-bodied instruments, such as the Montego, LTD, and Starcaster, but none of these managed to find a niche.

Bronco (1967)

Available only in the red finish pictured here, the Bronco was launched in 1968 and featured a single-coil pickup like the ones on Stratocasters. This instrument was discontinued in 1982.

Coronado II (1967)

The Coronado was one of Fender's rare hollow-bodied electric models. This guitar, the same width as Gibson's thinline models, appeared in the catalog in 1966. The instrument here features a special finish called "Wildwood," which follows the wood grain. Fender bought the patent for this finish from a Scandinavian chemist who discovered the process by injecting colored solutions into living beech trees. Once cut, the wood displayed spectacular designs that Fender put to good use on this model, as well as on their acoustic flat-top, the Kingman.

Jaguar (1964)

Like the Jazzmaster, the Jaguar was a high-quality model whose success was overshadowed by the Stratocaster's. Equipped with two Stratocaster-type pick-ups, a mute device, and a floating vibrato like the one found on the Jazzmaster, the Jaguar was a very upscale guitar. (In fact, it was once the most expensive Fenders available.) It was not widely popular in its time, but is being rediscovered today. The model shown here has a beautiful Candy Apple Red finish.

Les Paul:
~ A ~
Visionary

American guitar history has been shaped by a mere handful of major figures, and Les Paul must undoubtedly be counted among these men responsible for revolutionizing modern popular music. His artistic contributions, however, tend to be forgotten today. Many people don't realize that Les Paul was a real guitar hero in his own time. His talents as a guitar player alone should qualify him as a musical legend, but, on top of that, he was an electronic genius as well. Like Leo Fender, Les Paul was an inspired handyman who often transformed venerable old instruments into nightmarish creations covered with knobs, pick-ups, gadgets, and yards of wire, always for the sake of experimentation. But unlike his rival, Les Paul did not have to solicit the opinions of musicians to find out how his inventions worked, as he himself was an outstanding instrumentalist. Many of his ideas were ahead of their time, and he was often regarded as a likable, though somewhat eccentric, character. The fact that Les Paul persevered, that his revolutionary ideas were finally validated, and that the model bearing his name became one of the most popular in the world cannot be explained by any sort of business plan or marketing strategy, but only by sheer passion. This same passion is still driving Les Paul in the 1990s; he still regularly performs in New York night clubs at a time of his life when his substantial royalties might have otherwise enticed him to rest on his laurels under the Florida sun. The success of the Les Paul models encouraged Gibson to break away from its traditional designs and paved the way for the futuristic models that the company started to introduce in the late 1950s

Precision mechanics, a streamlined profile: the Les Paul, more than any other model, prefigures the guitar of the twenty-first century.

"Rhubarb Red":

alias Lester Polfus, alias Les Paul

Les Paul and Mary Ford.

Les Paul, originally Lester William Polfus, has spanned this century with a guitar in hand. Born in Wisconsin in 1916, he started his career in his teens, under the pseudonym "Rhubarb Red," and played a mixture of jazz and rhythm and blues in local clubs and radio stations.

He soon also displayed a talent for electronics, and the amplification of his guitar became an all-absorbing obsession. Even the family telephone and radio were victims of his early experiments. The young Lester dismantled the telephone one day and connected its primitive pickup to his guitar. This was plugged into Mom and Dad's precious radio. It was a long way from the sound of a solid-body plugged into a Marshall, but it was a promising beginning nonetheless. Les Paul was still a teenager when Rickenbacker, and then Gibson, came out with their first electric models, and the young guitar player followed the evolution of the new technology with great interest.

By the start of the war, Les Paul was a renowned instrumentalist who led his own trio at major events nationwide. He was already toying with the idea of a guitar of solid-wood construction, without a soundbox, to solve the feedback problems connected with the traditional hollow-body electric guitar. Around 1940, he started spending time at the Epiphone factory every weekend and began building his first prototype. He used a rectangular piece of wood onto which he affixed the pickups and the electronics, and to which he added a neck and two symmetri-

cal wings. (The wings were actually two halves of an Epiphone body, and were added only for aesthetics.) This prototype, since nicknamed "The Log" and now on display at the Country Music Hall of Fame in Nashville, was for many years Les Paul's touring companion, along with two similar models he made soon afterward. The musician presented these early prototypes to the Gibson directors, but all they earned him was a number of sarcastic remarks. He decided to focus on his performing career instead, and

he became a great success. He appeared with many major artists of the day, such as Bing Crosby, and recorded instrumental tracks that hit the charts. He then hooked up with singer Mary Ford, and formed one of the most popular musical duos of the 1950s.

In light of Les Paul's growing celebrity, as well as Fender's success with its first solid-body guitars, the Gibson people began to reconsider their initial opinion. Maurice Berlin, who was then the head of CMI, Gibson's parent company, put his people to work: "Find me that guy with the broomstick with pickups on it!"

The innovator's signature appears on all Les Paul models.

Les Paul and Mary Ford

Les Paul and Mary Ford formed one of America's most popular post-war duos. Les Paul, like Leo Fender, was a great tinkerer, and most of the guitars that Gibson lent him show traces of his constant experiments.

Obviously, Les Paul, who often topped the music charts with Mary Ford in those days, wasn't hard to find.

Once they made contact, Les Paul presented all the requests and ideas that he had had time to develop, and the Gibson engineers went to work. A prototype was created, and an official meeting finally took place in the presence of lawyers from both parties. Les Paul signed a contract guaranteeing him five percent of the sales of the model bearing his name. He probably didn't realize it then, but he had just secured himself a very comfortable retirement. Forty-five years later, the Les Paul remains, along with the Fender Stratocaster, the world's most popular solid-body model.

The Gold Top

An Overnight Success

The first Les Paul came out of the Gibson factory in the spring of 1952, two years after Fender launched the Broadcaster. How much of this new concept was due to Les Paul, and how much due to the Gibson think tank? The debate is still open, each contributor naturally claiming the greater responsibility for such a successful model. It seems likely that the gold finish was Les Paul's idea, as he shamelessly admits to his fondness for a little gaudiness. On the other hand, Maurice Berlin, a great violin aficionado, probably came up with the concept of the two-part body: a mahogany base and a solid, convex maple table that resembled that of an arch-top guitar. The Gibson company, already experts at this type of gui-

tar construction, thus greatly reduced the chances of being copied as their competitors had neither the know-how nor the proper equipment to carve such tops. Furthermore, the combination of maple and mahogany probably had a substantial effect on the sound of these instruments, the woods being wonderfully complementary in terms of acous-

tic qualities. As far as electronics were concerned, the new Gibson model borrowed a system already found on several jazz models: that is, a couple of single-coil pickups, called P90s. The Les Paul was nevertheless far from perfect, its main weakness being the position of the neck which was attached on the same plane as the body. Guitars should generally have a slight

increase in the neck's height to compensate for the angle imposed on the strings by the height of the bridge. The result of this unfortunate imperfection was that the strings, instead of running on top of the bridge-tailpiece combination invented by Les Paul, had to be placed under it in order to attain a reasonable height. This was clearly a mistake. A very dissatisfied Les Paul, in 1953, convinced Gibson to improve the neck by setting it at a more appropriate angle. Also, the trapeze-shaped tailpiece was replaced by a stud tailpiece that greatly improved the sustain of the instrument. Two years later, the famous Tune-o-Matic bridge, which made it possible to

adjust the intonation of each individual string, appeared on this model. In 1953, Gibson also experimented by launching a new model: the Les Paul Custom, for which the guitarist came up with the idea of an all black finish—to match to his tuxedo!

Les Paul Custom Prototype (1953)

According to its owner, Lars Henrikson, this guitar is one of the few prototypes (there were probably five) of the Les Paul Custom, which was officially launched in 1954. Gibson used to release a few units of each model so that all the employees—technicians, craftsmen, repairmen, salesmen—could contribute their comments before a model was actually launched. This model is almost identical to the production ones released the following year, the top simply curved in a slightly different way.

Les Paul Gold Top (1954)

Often called a "Gold Top" by today's guitar enthusiasts because of its finish, this model, the first of the Les Paul series, was officially called the "Les Paul Model." Originally equipped with an ill-conceived trapeze tailpiece, the model was modified in 1953. The original tailpiece was replaced with this cylindrical combination of bridge and tailpiece, directly affixed to the top. The Gold Top disappeared in 1958 and was replaced by the Les Paul Standard, but it would reappear in the Gibson catalog ten years later.

Early Variations

Luxury and Budget Versions

Launched in 1954, the Custom—with its black finish, multiple bindings, rectangular fingerboard inlays, peghead enhanced with the famous split-diamond inlay, and gold-plated accents—looks much classier than the Gold Top. In addition to sporting this luxury look, the new model was also a vehicle for two Gibson innovations. First, unusually low frets allowed for comfortable left hand fingering. This feature, which let the player's fingers slide effortlessly up and down the neck, explains why the Custom was nicknamed "The Fretless Wonder." Second, the guitar was equipped with a P90 pickup on the bridge side, like its sibling the Gold Top, and also with a new type of pickup—called an "Alnico" because of the aluminum-nickel-cobalt composition of its magnets—which was supposed to have more power than its predecessors. With the Custom also appeared a new type of bridge, called a Tune-o-Matic, which allowed the player to individually adjust the length of each string, thereby ensuring that they would be properly tuned. This type of bridge was also found on the Gold Top beginning in 1955. Another major difference between the two models was the method of their body construc-

tion. Unlike the Gold Top which, as we learned, was built of a sandwich of mahogany and maple, the Custom was built from a single mahogany block, giving it a mellower tone that Les Paul seemed to prefer.

Starting in 1954, Gibson offered, along with the Custom, the Les Paul Junior, a more economical model with a plainer silhouette. Though it had a shape similar to that of its predecessors, the Junior did not share their arched top, but rather featured a flat top just like the rival Fender Telecaster. Equipped with a single P90 pickup and sporting the traditional sunburst finish, the Junior, with its minimal decoration, was obviously targeting beginners on a budget.

That same year a similar model came out—this one with a natural finish—and it was called the Les Paul TV in honor of the many televised appearances of Les Paul and Mary Ford. One might wonder, however, if its name wasn't a direct allusion to the Telecaster, which happened to have the exact same finish and price. This series of economical models was rounded out by the Special, which was equipped with two pickups.

Between 1958 and 1959 the silhouettes of the Junior, the TV, and the Special changed, since around that time Gibson was introducing the double cutaway, which gave the player access to the highest frets on the neck.

Les Paul TV 3/4 (1954)

The Les Paul TV was actually a Junior with a blonde finish, which was better-looking on television in the black-and-white era. Launched in 1954, only five Les Paul TV guitars were produced that year, and this one is probably the first to feature a short-scale neck, a characteristic more common on TV models after 1956.

Les Paul Junior (ca. 1960)

Beginning in 1958, Gibson changed the shape of the Les Paul Junior—as well as that of the Special and the TV—resulting in this modern silhouette with exceptional access to the highest part of the fingerboard. The guitar was still an economical model, with a single pickup, a flat top (as opposed to Les Paul models with arched tops), and little ornamentation. The same year, Gibson replaced the sunburst on this popular model (one of the company's biggest sellers) with a cherry finish.

Les Paul Custom (1955)

When it was launched in 1954, the Les Paul Custom did not go unnoticed, firstly because of its price (325 dollars) which was quite a sum in those days, but mostly because of its beautiful black finish, its rectangular inlays, and its adorned peghead. It was also the first Les Paul to have a Tune-o-Matic bridge, which allowed the length of each string to be adjusted individually, thus improving the guitar's fine tuning. The Custom also introduced a new pickup (the "Alnico") in the neck position; the lead pickup remained a P90 like that on the Les Paul Gold Top

The Sunburst

The Collector's Holy Grail

In the early 1950s, Gibson hired Seth Lover, an electronics specialist who played an important role in the company's development of the Alnico pickups that would equip the Les Paul Custom. Although this was quite an accomplishment, it was the challenge he faced toward the end of the decade that would make him a legend in the guitar world.

The Gibson directors were dissatisfied with the effectiveness of their single-coil pickups. Up until then, the company, like most of its competitors, used this type of pickup on their instruments despite its one major drawback: an annoying tendency to pick up electrical interferences, which turned into a hum as the guitar's volume increased. Seth Lover was asked to develop a pickup that would eliminate this undesirable humming noise. He succeeded perfectly and called the result of his research a "humbucker." This new pickup was made with two coils (instead of one as on earlier pickups) with opposite magnetic polarities, which, in musical terms, simply translated to a bigger, rounder sound, with no extraneous noise. The revolutionary pickup, which was covered with an isolated metal plate, first appeared on the Les Paul Gold Top and Custom in 1957, but, unfortunately, could not keep the sales of these models from plummeting.

To counter the public's temporary dissatisfaction, Gibson decided to change the look of the Les Paul. The designers thought it might be inter-esting to take advantage of the beauty of the maple top, and so they decided to enhance it with a sunburst finish that would accentuate the wood's grain. Starting in 1958, the tops of Les Pauls were carefully constructed in two parts (Gold Tops were often built with three-part tops), with the wood meticulously book-matched, as on a violin. These guitars, built between 1958 and 1960, and cataloged by Gibson as Les Paul Standards (and by collectors as "Sunbursts" or "Bursts") are among the most coveted solid-bodies today. They command astronomical prices, probably more because of the beauty of their maple tops than because of their musical qualities.

The first factory pickups used on these instruments had a sticker on their base that read "Patent Applied For." These pickups, today called "PAFs," are also in high demand among collectors. The uninitiated listener will now understand why a conversation between aficionados about a "Burst with PAF" is certain to be animated. He will also realize that we have now left the music world for the more elusive world of "collectomania."

Gary Moore and the Les Paul Sunburst

Guitarist Gary Moore owns a famous sunburst that had earlier belonged to Peter Green. (Moore produced, in 1997, a tribute album to his fellow Englishman using this guitar.) Over time this model lost, as did many instruments of similar vintage, the red component of its original sunburst and now sports a rather plain, light-brown finish that collectors cleverly refer to as an "unburst." Other famous guitarists, like Jeff Beck, Eric Clapton, and Duane Allman, have used Les Paul Standards. Today they are so valuable that they can be found more frequently in the homes or bank vaults of collectors than in the hands of musicians. The Sunburst, along with the Flying V and Loar-signed instruments, is one of the most copied guitars in the world, and counterfeits are not unusual.

During the two years of its production, the Sunburst underwent only a few minor changes: the thin frets of the 1950s were replaced by larger ones in mid-1959, and the neck was made slightly thinner in 1960.

Gibson SG

A Les Paul—without Les Paul

In 1961, the Les Paul Junior, Standard, and Custom were given new looks. Now sporting a double cutaway, these models were easily recognized by their two "horns," which were a hit with the public of the day. It seems that Les Paul himself, however, was not won over; he once told journalist Tom Wheeler: "You could kill yourself on horns like that!" These models are today called SG/Les Paul by collectors, but in 1963, Les Paul actually had his name removed the model. Officially, this was because he was in the process of separating from Mary Ford, and since his contract with Gibson

was up, he did not want to renew it until the divorce was settled. One might safely assume, however, that his dissatisfaction with the new look of his favorite model was part of the reason he withdrew his endorsement.

The SG was quite successful anyway, but ironically, throughout the 1960s, musicians such as Eric Clapton, Keith Richards, and Jimmy Page were pulling out their old Sunburst Standards, thus putting them back in vogue with the public. Guitarists all around the world, wanting

to emulate their idols, started looking for instruments produced at the end of the 1950s, and in doing so began history's first vintage guitar craze. Consumer demand finally persuaded the Gibson company to restore the original look of the Les Paul. In 1967, they once again hooked up with Les Paul, and a new

contract was drawn up—this one guaranteeing the artist six dollars for every model sold. The reissue models had the same features as the 1950s Gibsons. The Custom (with two pickups) and the Gold Top led the way in 1968, followed by an array of Les Pauls for every taste and almost every budget: the 1969 Deluxe with mini-humbuckers; the Signature with a hollow body like a 335; the various Anniversary models; the beautifully ornate Artisan of the late 1970s; as well as several other models still being reissued today. The Les Paul, forty-five years later, is doing just fine, thank-you.

SG/Les Paul 1961 and 1962

In early 1961, Gibson changed the Les Paul shape to this rather unusual one. Until 1963, Les Paul endorsed the model, his signature appearing on the truss-rod cover, above the peghead nut. When he left Gibson in 1963, his name disappeared and the model was renamed the SG Standard. Note, on both these models, the Deluxe sideways vibrato, which was discontinued in 1963.

Les Paul Silverburst (1981)

At this time the Les Paul, which was about to celebrate its thirtieth anniversary, was losing popularity, the 1980s being dominated by the sound of single-coils. Gibson desperately tried to recapture the attention of its public, and this silver finish was one of many attempts in that direction, as well as a move toward a more contemporary look. In an opposite vein, that same year, the company introduced its Heritage Series which recaptured its past with facsimiles of its vintage models.

Les Paul Historic Flametop (1996)

The Gibson company, like most major guitar manufacturers, understood the advantages of reissuing its most popular models. Why let the vintage dealers be the only ones to reap the profits of its former glory? One of the best recent success stories in this area was Gibson's launch of the Historic Collection. The series boasts twenty or so of its most classic models, including eight different Les Pauls. The Les Paul Flametop is a copy of the Les Paul Standard from 1960, and its top is carved in a curly maple that is often superior to that of the originals.

The Flying V

A Supersonic Guitar

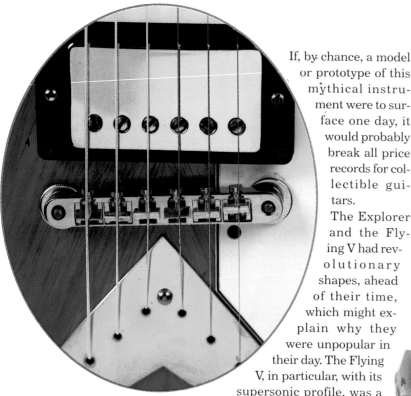

When Gibson decided to produce guitars to target a younger clientele (who up until this time tended to prefer Gretsch or Fender products), they put their own engineers, as well as outside designers, to work. The latter came up with a whole series of ideas for futuristic-looking guitars. Considering that only the most pragmatic, feasible, and easily produced ideas were chosen, one can imagine how outrageous some of the rejected concepts might have been.

If, by chance, a model or prototype of this mythical instrument were to surface one day, it would probably break all price records for collectible guitars.

The Explorer and the Flying V had revolutionary shapes, ahead of their time, which might explain why they were unpopular in their day. The Flying V, in particular, with its supersonic profile, was a beautiful, streamlined guitar, though an awkward one to play. With this model, the Gibson company finally broke away from its conservative reputation, though they couldn't seem to convince the public, despite the publicity they received from bluesmen Lonnie Mack and Albert King, who both adopted the instrument, probably because of its convenient access to all twenty-two frets. Although these Modernistic Guitars, as Gibson called them, were a failure when they were launched, it would not be long before they acquired a legendary status. This new-found status, not surprisingly, motivated Gibson to develop a number of reissues and compelled its competitors to produce copies.

At the end of the 1950s, Gibson launched a series of three futuristic-looking guitars: the Flying V, the Explorer, and the Moderne. All of these were made from korina, an African wood which Gibson had previously used for lap-steels, and which resembles mahogany, although it is lighter in color. The first two models, launched in 1958, were dismal failures. Only ninety-eight Flying Vs and twenty-two Explorers were built between 1958 and 1959 according to the company's log book, though it's likely that a few unrecorded models were built in the early 1960s.

As for the Moderne, it's the instrument everyone talks about but no one has seen—except in the original copyright drawing.

Flying V (1958)

The 1958 Gibson catalog introduced the Flying V as the perfect choice for an artist seeking a theatrical image; what it did not mention was that the instrument was particularly difficult to handle because of its unusual profile and its annoying lack of balance. A piece of rubber was even attached to the back of the guitar to prevent the guitar from sliding against the musician as he played. Nonetheless, these minor inconveniences don't keep collectors from fighting over the few rare copies on the market.

The Firebird and Explorer:
More Gibson Solid-bodies

Gibson produced many other solid-body models. Among the most important is the Firebird series, launched in 1963. Once again, these were guitars designed to compete with Fender products, which were slowly becoming the leaders in the solid-body market. Cautious after the disastrous Modernistic Guitar experience, the Gibson executives now had to try to incorporate some forward-thinking qualities into their new models without alienating their rather conservative clientele. To this end, they recruited the talents of automobile designer Ray Dietrich, who came up with the Firebird, a model that resembled the Fender Jazzmaster. Its construction was specially conceived, however, since Gibson wanted to avoid the Fender method of building the body and the neck separately. Bigsby and Rickenbacker had experimented with a new method a few years earlier, and Gibson decided to try a similar one. For the Firebird, a single piece of wood was used for the neck and the center part of the body. (Though this "piece of wood" was actually two pieces of mahogany glued together to prevent potential warping.) Pickups, a bridge, and a tailpiece were attached, and two "wings" were then added to the whole. This new construction method had two major advantages: it enabled the company to save their wider, more expensive pieces of wood, and it also improved the sustain and the vibration of the instrument.

The Firebird also featured a new, smaller humbucker, with non-adjustable pole pieces. Four models came out in 1963, each model's name being followed by an odd Roman numeral: I, III, V, or VII, depending on the level of ornamentation. Because of the pressures of competition, these guitars could be ordered in custom colors, a first at Gibson. Unfortunately, the threat of a lawsuit with Fender (who found the newcomer's look a little too reminiscent of the Jazzmaster) coupled with a rather cool public reception, compelled Gibson to cease production of this superb series in 1965. The Gibson company was, therefore, ultimately unsuccessful at promoting its vision of the guitar of the future.

Since the 1970s, Gibson has launched many other solid-body models, with varying success. Some examples are the L-5S, a solid-body version of the famed jazz-guitar; the L-6S; the Marauder; and the Nighthawk. The company also collaborated with country guitar player Chet Atkins to produce, in the 1980s, a superb solid-body guitar with nylon strings, which at last allowed classical guitarists to rival the decibel levels of heavy metal bands.

Gibson Firebird III (1968)

When the Firebird appeared in 1963, its body and head had the reverse profile of the model shown here, which looks like its mirror image. The instruments from this initial series are now known as Reverse-Body Firebirds. After 1965, the model adopted a "Non-Reverse" shape, and other notable changes occurred at the same time. Most importantly, the solid wood block construction for the neck and central body was abandoned for a traditional neck–body junction. The Firebird III was equipped with three P90 pickups.

L-6S Deluxe

The L-6S was a simplified version of the L-5S, which was a solid-body version of the L-5. This unusual model offered several characteristics rarely associated with Gibsons: a yellow metallic finish, a maple fingerboard, and strings passing through the body and anchored on the back instead of on the tailpiece. The two latter characteristics are similar to those on Fender instruments, which Gibson was probably trying to emulate. The L-6S, which appeared in the mid-1970s, disappeared from the Gibson catalog in 1980.

Gibson Explorer (1976)

The Explorer was initially launched in 1958 as part of the Modernistic Guitar series (see page 120), and its shape at that time was as revolutionary as that of the Flying V. It was, however, a failure and was officially discontinued in 1959 (although a few units were still produced in the early 1960s). Since then, the Explorer has been reintroduced many times, in different versions and with new modifications. This particular model was part of the first series of reissues, launched in 1975. It differs from the original mainly in that it is built of mahogany rather than korina. This model is available in a natural, black, or white finish.

More Great
～ Guitars ～
Makers

During the second half of the twentieth century, the world of popular music was dominated largely by Americans. It's only logical, then, that American guitar builders claimed the largest share of the worldwide market over that period of time. It was also natural that Fender, Martin, and Gibson be at the top of the industry since the international media paid most attention to musical genres—such as pop, rock, blues, jazz, and country—that were strongly tied to American culture. Fortunately, however, the presence of these three major players was not exclusive, and there are some notable exceptions to their dominance. British bands, though they have obviously shown a preference for the instruments of the "big three," have also been responsible for popularizing more obscure models, like Gretsch and Rickenbacker, and British guitars and amps like those of Vox or Marshall. It is also interesting to note that the Asians, so far known mainly for producing copies and for accommodating the relocation of plants of major companies, might one day surprise us all by offering models that could rival American-made ones. All this diversification is not only inevitable, but also highly desirable. The guitar, ever-present in today's music, can only benefit from a widening variety of international cultures, know-how, and technology.

Vox was able to capitalize on the predominance of British rock in the 1960s.

Gretsch

The Dance of Colors

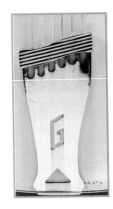

Gretsch's story is unique. Its products, often criticized by those who love precision and abhor gadgets, are nevertheless the only ones that can seriously rival the guitars of the "big three": Martin, Fender, and Gibson. Gretsch's guitars—showy, covered in a constantly changing variety of doodads, and available in eye-catching finishes—do have their ardent defenders. Considering the caliber of guitarists who have been associated with the company (Chet Atkins, George Harrison, Brian Setzer, Dave Stewart, Duane Eddy), it is obvious that Gretsch played an important role in the evolution of the guitar in the second half of the century.

Founded in 1883, the Gretsch company started out building banjos and drums before switching to arch-top guitars in the 1930s, concentrating on a line of acoustic instruments called the Synchromatics. With the exception of a few models built before the war, it wasn't until the early 1950s that Gretsch seriously converted to electricity; this is when the company started to produce instruments that made an immediate public impact. Such was the case with the Electromatic, a 16-inch guitar with a cutaway and one or two pickups. But the real revolution occurred when Gretsch hired Jimmie Webster, an immensely talented musician (who first introduced "tapping," a technique revived by rock musicians in the 1980s). Webster completely changed the face of the old company and proposed several new concepts that appeared on a line of instruments launched in 1955. Many of Webster's innovations were an

Gretsch Double Anniversary (1964)

Launched in 1958 to celebrate the company's seventy-fifth year in business, the Anniversary started out with two FilterTron pickups. This model was especially noted for its attractive "two-tone smoke green" finish, with the back and sides sporting a darker shade of green than the top. Starting in 1960, the guitar was equipped with two Hi-Lo Tron pickups. The model was discontinued in 1975.

immediate success, in particular the bold finishes that decorated most of the models. In those days, Fender was not yet offering its selection of "custom colors," so the first Chet Atkins, Streamliner, and Country Club models that Gretsch launched, with their orange, green, yellow, or black finishes, instantly attracted a young audience thrilled to find a new way to shock their elders. The White Falcon, the most expensive of the line, was particularly remarkable. With its white finish, peghead adorned with a glittering, golden falcon, bindings of similar material, and its V-shaped tailpiece (called a Cadillac Tailpiece by collectors), it remains, forty years after its inception, one of the kitschiest guitars ever built and certainly one of the most sought after. Gretsch's continued success, then, was due mainly to the popularity of its arch-top models. Its solid-body guitars (see pages 132 and 133) were less well received. Oddly enough, however, their White Penguin (a solid-body version of the White Falcon) is probably the most expensive solid-body on the vintage market today.

In 1967, Gretsch was sold to Baldwin by the founder's family. This hastened the decline of the company, which then started to produce larger guitars and pushed the addition of silly gadgets to absurd extremes.

In 1985, the company was bought back by Fred Gretsch III, who, with the help of Duke Kramer, put the venerable house back on track. At first they relocated their operations abroad, but

later an American factory was opened again. The new team resurrected the old Gretsch models, as well as the FilterTron and DeArmond pickups that equipped them. This move proved very successful, and the Gretsch guitars made today have the reputation (deservedly so) of being superior to those built in the fifties. This turna-round has had quite an effect on the vintage market, surprising many speculators who thought they had found, in guitars, a safe way to invest their extra dollars (or yen).

Gretsch Streamliner 6190 (1955)

The Gretsch catalog is unusually complex, with models constantly changing names over the years. This guitar is part of the Electromatic series, whose first models appeared in 1940, and the series name is clearly marked on the peghead. Nevertheless, the block fingerboard inlays, the bindings around the f-holes and the top, the presence of a single DeArmond pickup, and the Gretsch tailpiece stamped with a "G" all would indicate that this instrument is a Streamliner 6190. This particular model, whose production started in 1955, was discontinued in 1959. It reappeared in 1969 with a new look.

Gretsch Streamliner 6102 (ca. 1970)

In the 1960s, Gretsch offered a series of thinner guitars, similar to the Gibson thinlines, such as the Viking, Rally, and Streamliner. (A few years earlier, there was also a standard-sized guitar called a Streamliner.) The model shown here features some of the many Gretsch innovations, for example, the unusual roller bridge. It also has a unique fret system on the highest part of the neck (called the "T-zone"), which was supposed to improve the tone of the instrument.

Gretsch 6120

From Chet Atkins to Brian Setzer

Jimmie Webster was one of the first executives at the Gretsch company to realize the importance of the Gibson–Les Paul association and to dream about a similar arrangement. His company had used a few celebrity guitarists in their advertising campaigns, of course, but none of them had the stature of Gibson's protégé, and more importantly, none had collaborated directly on the conception and construction of an instrument. Webster decided that Chet Atkins would be his man.

Even in the early 1950s, the young Atkins was a nationally known guitarist, and his country style, inherited from Merle Travis, was immensely popular in the South. Chet Atkins' music was simple and melodic, appealing to the general public, but, at the same time, it was technically advanced enough to impress guitar players. Webster managed (with much difficulty) to convince Fred Gretsch Jr., who was then running the company, to let him try a collaboration with the Nashville musician, and he was put in charge of organizing it himself. It turned out to be a long and difficult process.

Atkins was not convinced as to the quality of the instruments presented to him, and his list of requests would go on and on. At long last, he and Webster agreed upon a design for a prototype that was built in 1954. The guitar made an impression as soon as it was launched, Gretsch taking full advantage of promoting its country image. Its design was,

in fact, to the point of caricature, and though it might appeal to many today because of its kitschy, retro look, Atkins had a hard time swallowing that western pill. The model featured a cattle horn on the peghead, cactus motifs on the inlays, and a G "branded" on the table. All this appeared on an arch-top body equipped with two DeArmond pickups and adorned with an orange finish: it was daring, to say the least. For his part, Atkins managed to persuade the reluctant Gretsch company to include a Bigsby vibrato on the instrument. At the same time, Gretsch launched a solid-body version that did poorly, but the arch-top model, called the Chet Atkins Hollow Body (number 6120 in the catalog), was every bit as successful as were Atkins' albums for RCA in those days. Gradually, the western characteristics of this model started to disappear, and, in 1957, the DeArmond pickups that Atkins so disliked were replaced by FilterTrons, inspired by Gibson humbuckers.

The success of this first model encouraged the company to expand upon its collaborations with Chet Atkins in 1958. Two new guitars were launched that year: the Country Gentleman (the guitarist's nickname) and the Tennessean. The former was an upscale model that sold for 525 dollars, quite a sum in those days. Despite its cost, it was a great success thanks to its simple shape, mahogany finish, impressive 17-inch size, and its body featuring fake soundholes simply painted on. This model—

which greatly benefited from the publicity it received through George Harrison, who played one while the Beatles were at the peak of their popularity—was one of Gretsch's best sellers. The Tennessean, with its cherry finish, was a more economical model, equipped with a single pickup. These guitars all went through many changes over the years,

and more models connected with Chet Atkins were later released, such as the Super Chet, in 1972, and the Super Axe in 1977. Despite all this success, the collaboration between the guitarist-producer and the company, one of the richest in the history of music, ended in 1978, twenty-five years after it was initiated. Chet Atkins then defected to the enemy: Gibson.

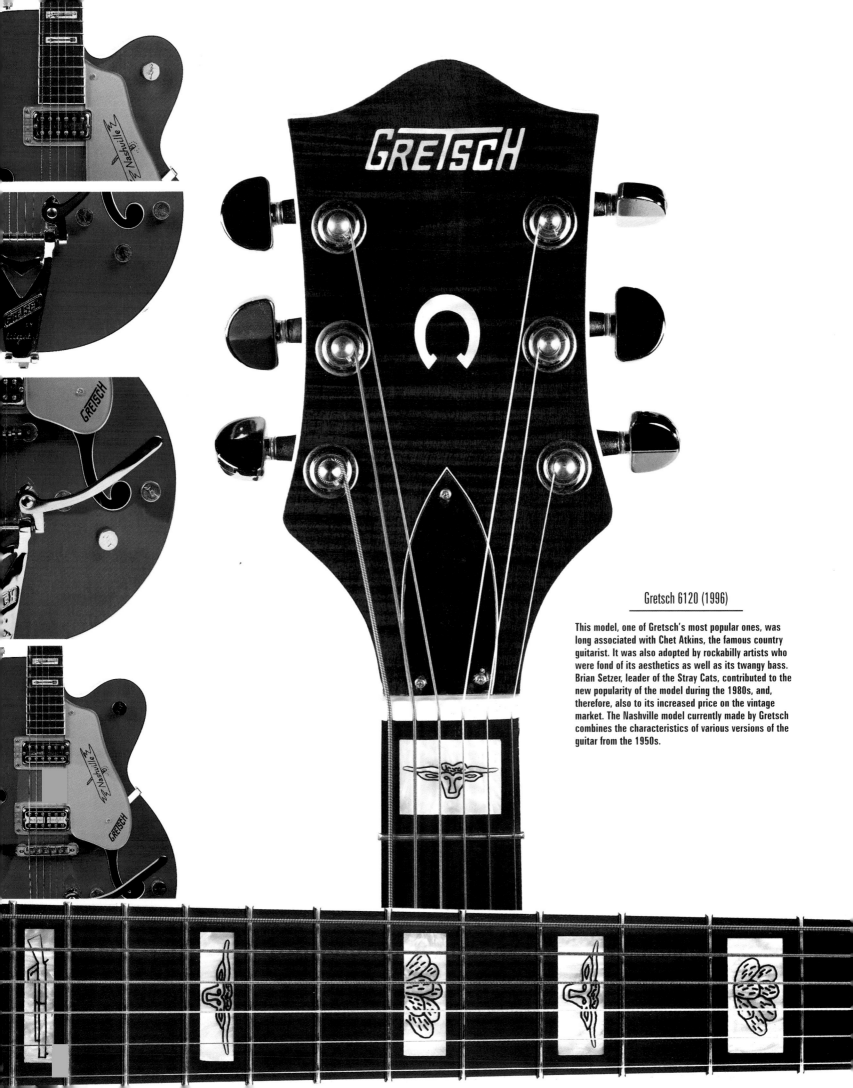

Gretsch 6120 (1996)

This model, one of Gretsch's most popular ones, was long associated with Chet Atkins, the famous country guitarist. It was also adopted by rockabilly artists who were fond of its aesthetics as well as its twangy bass. Brian Setzer, leader of the Stray Cats, contributed to the new popularity of the model during the 1980s, and, therefore, also to its increased price on the vintage market. The Nashville model currently made by Gretsch combines the characteristics of various versions of the guitar from the 1950s.

Rickenbacker

Small Fish in a Big Pond

The Rickenbacker company, founded in 1925 by a Swiss immigrant of the same name, initially built metal objects of all sorts. But soon, its association with National enticed its directors to give the guitar market, then in full bloom, a try. This new activity expanded, particularly when George Beauchamp (see pages 84 and 85), who had left National, found at Rickenbacker the ideal atmosphere in which to develop his electric guitar concepts. That's how a new series of instruments, first under the brand Electro String Instruments, and then under Rickenbacker, came out. This, starting in 1932, opened a new chapter in guitar history.

The company initially concentrated mostly on lap-steels; then, after a pause due to the war effort, it was sold in 1953 by its founder to Radio-Tel, a distributor of electronic devices that already had Fender under its wing. Under the direction of this new owner, Rickenbacker concentrated his efforts on the guitar, launching solid-bodies as early as 1954 with the Combo series. These models had a unique shape that made them stand apart from the other hip guitars of the day, Fenders and Les Pauls. The first Combo featured a "horseshoe" pickup (this continued until 1959) similar to the one Rickenbacker used on its lap-steel. This pickup, with its characteristic shape, enveloped the strings from the upper side, so that they were placed in the magnetic field.

These guitars are especially sought after by collectors nowadays. In 1957, the company hired Roger Rossmeil, a German-born designer who later worked for Gibson, to develop the Capri series. These guitars were adopted by the Beatles (in particular, John Lennon, who played a 325), which greatly enhanced the company's image. The Capris were reminiscent of thinline models such as the Gibson 335; their hollow-bodies and similar reduced depth would definitely classify them in this category. Nevertheless, true to its reputation as a non-conformist, Rickenbacker introduced several changes that made the guitars different from those of its competitors (for example, a relatively thicker soundboard, heavy braces, and minimal soundholes)—and almost qualified them as solid-bodies. The Capri series was organized by way of a complex number system, ranging from 310 to 375. Models 310 to 325 had a shorter scale, those from 330 to 345 a standard scale, and those from 360 to 375 a standard scale and "deluxe" ornamentation. Within each series, the models, designated by numbers spaced apart by fives (for example: 310, 315, 320), differentiated themselves by the number of pickups they possessed and by the presence or absence of a vibrato.

Rickenbacker, a small company in terms of production, had, nonetheless, an important impact on the guitar world. The brand has both its supporters and its detractors, each just as adamant as the other.

Rickenbacker Combo 400 (ca. 1957)

In 1956, Rickenbacker introduced a line of instruments truly ahead of its time. These guitars, shaped roughly like a tulip, were constructed from a single block of wood used for the neck and the central part of the body. (This concept was used by Gibson for the Firebird a few years later.) This model, called the Combo 400, is decorated in a "cloverfield green" finish. Note that the aluminum pickguard covers most of the body.

Rickenbacker Combo 450 (1960)

Starting in 1958, Rickenbacker's tulip-shaped solid-body gave way to this longer silhouette dubbed the "cresting wave" by their designers. The large metallic pickguard of the older models is still present.

Rickenbacker 360 WB (ca. 1985)

The 360, launched in 1958, was characterized by its two pickups and its triangular fingerboard inlays. After 1964, the shape of the cutaway was changed. (See the 360-12 model.) The original models were reissued in 1984.

Rickenbacker 360-12 (1990)

The Rickenbacker Capri (or 300) series has always been one of the builder's most popular. The 12-string models were particularly in demand, thanks, firstly, to George Harrison, who used one on the Beatles' hit "A Hard Day's Night," and, secondly, to Roger McGuinn, who popularized the instrument while playing with The Byrds

Rickenbacker 615 (1967)

The 615 had a body similar to that of the Combo 450, but, unlike the latter, was also equipped with a vibrato. Note that the aluminum pickguard of the earlier models has been replaced by a much smaller plastic one.

The Outsiders

Minor Brands, Major Achievements

Although the majority of quality solid-body guitars has been produced by Fender and Gibson, those made throughout the years by other makers, which were often very decent, should not be ignored. Some of these guitar builders have already been mentioned for their arch-tops; for example, Gretsch, who happened to also produce outrageously designed solid-bodies. The company started offering solid-bodies in 1953, only three years after the launch of the first Fender Broadcaster (a name which, as we have learned, Fender had to relinquish because of Gretsch's previous copyright on it).

The same year, the Duo-Jet came out, featuring two single-coil DeArmond pickups, and especially noted for its bold finish. It was covered with a black synthetic material, previously used only to cover drum kits. When the Silver-Jet was launched in 1954, the company pushed its provocative use of color one step further by introducing a metallic silver finish. These innovations most certainly encouraged Fender to launch its own custom color models. The White Penguin,

a solid-body version of the White Falcon, with a similar stunning white finish, was launched in 1955. It remains one of the most sought-after guitars of all time. In the late 1950s, Gretsch launched another series of solid-bodies endorsed by Bo Diddley. Then in 1969, the Roc Jet, Gretsch's answer to the Gibson Les Paul, appeared. Guild and Epiphone, two companies known more for their arch-top guitars, also make a humble appearance in solid-body history. In the 1960s, Guild produced several

solid-bodies, such as the Polara and the Thunderbird. Later, drawing inspiration largely from Gibson, it launched the M and S lines, before giving up the production of solid-bodies altogether in 1989. Similarly, Epiphone produced, in the early 1960s, a series of these instruments that included the Coronet, the Olympic, the Crestwood Custom, and the Crestwood Deluxe. The latter model was the most ornate of the series, equipped with three mini-

humbuckers and with the trademark Epiphone vibrato, the Trem-o-Tone.

Mosrite, on the other hand, is one of those legendary builders that is revered by guitar aficionados, but was never really appreciated by the general public. This Californian company, founded by Semie Moseley, had its moment of glory in the 1960s when artists like the Monkees and country guitarist Joe Maphis popularized its instruments on their TV shows.

Martin GT-75

The Martin company is so famous for its acoustic models that many guitar fans forget that it also built both arch-top and solid-body electric guitars. The GT-75 is from the former category. Launched in 1965, it features two cutaways and a vibrato. Note that the shape of the model's peghead is quite different from that of Martin's acoustic instruments.

Guild T-100 DP (1961)

With its two pickups and minimal ornamentation, this model was a budget version of the Stuart 500. Guild, founded by Alfred Dronge in New York in 1952, hired many ex-workers from the Epiphone factory, who were specialists in arch-top construction. Therefore, the Guild company naturally produced high-quality instruments in this same style.

Mosrite Fantasy

Semie Moseley, who founded his company in the early 1960s, built guitars with very unusual shapes, that happened to be to the liking of California musicians such as Joe Maphis, the Monkees, and the Collins Kids. This model (which no

longer has its original finish) was one of the first built after Moseley resumed his operations after a fire destroyed his entire factory. This explains the use of the serial number AF 22 (the letters standing for "after fire").

Epiphone Crestwood Custom (ca. 1965)

Although this model first appeared in 1958, Epiphone offered this type of modern shape only after 1963. The off-waist body, the "batwing" peghead, the oval fingerboard inlays, and the mini-humbucker pickups make this quite a good-quality guitar, and an affordable one on today's vintage market.

Gretsch Roc Jet (1974)

Known mainly for its arch-top guitars, Gretsch also built solid-bodies, some of which, like the White Penguin, even reached legendary status. A more modest guitar, this Roc Jet, with its two SuperTron pickups, its adjustable bridge, and its "Mercedes Black" finish, is still a good example of the company's unique sense of aesthetics.

Vox, a surprising aesthetic

Surprisingly, few English guitar makers were able to capitalize on the predominance of British rock in the 1960s. Vox was one of the rare companies (along with Burns) able to benefit from this period. Vox probably owes most of its success to the unusual aesthetics of its instruments. From the Phantom series with its coffin shape, to the MK VI with its teardrop shape, Vox produced an impressive range of different models. Some had long-term success, but many others were short-lived, as was the case with other oddities like Vox's guitar-organ, an unusual hybrid with a guitar body and an organ sound. Vox's operations were relocated to Italy in the late 1960s.

The Modern Guitar

A New Revolution

O f all guitars styles, solid-bodies evolve the fastest and will most likely serve as models for the instruments of the twenty-first century. Acoustic arch-top and flat-top guitars seem to have stabilized at a standard size, and the materials used to construct them aren't likely to change much, unless their availability becomes a problem. If so, the woods that become scarce will simply be replaced by other, more easily obtainable ones. Some companies, like

Gibson, already fund reforestation and research programs in which biologists and forestry experts study the possibilities of growing future substitution woods. As for solid-bodies, however, anything seems possible. For a long time guitar makers have experimented with synthetic materials, and the future may even hold a new one that could make wood completely obsolete. Today, the use of modern materials like carbon fiber, Plexiglas, and all kinds of plastics is common—although this trend is not exactly new since in the

1960s, for example, National was already producing futuristic, fiberglass instruments that closely resemble the Metropolitans produced today.

Builders like Veleno in Florida, or James Trussard in France, even build solid-bodies made of metal. In the early 1980s Steinberger launched a revolutionary graphite bass, with a minimalist body and no head, the tuning being done at the tailpiece. More recently, Ken Parker has built very high-quality guitars of the same material, which have been well-received by many noted guitarists. Apart from these relatively rare futuristic versions, the most recent major technical improvements on solid-bodies occurred in the 1980s. One of the key figures in this revolution was Grover Jackson, who launched a line of instruments that was immediately adopted by many rock and heavy-metal musicians. These were the first guitars to make the Stratocaster actually look outdated. These instruments, which inspired an impressive array of clones, were similar in construction to Gibson Firebirds, with a single piece of wood being used for the neck and central body. This struc-

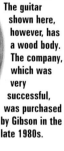

Schecter Original Californian Custom (1990s)

Simple and classic, this model has a top made of beautifully patterned curly maple. The Schecter company was one of the first to offer "customizable" models by selling parts that allowed the player to modify his instrument as he wished.

Steinberger GM 7

Founded in 1980 by engineer Ned Steinberger, the company was an overnight success thanks to the release of its headless basses (and then guitars) made of graphite, an epoxy resin reinforced with glass and carbon fibers. The guitar shown here, however, has a wood body. The company, which was very successful, was purchased by Gibson in the late 1980s.

Parker Fly (1996)

Created by Ken Parker, this model is one of the most innovative of the past twenty years. Remarkably light (less than six pounds), very thin, and futuristic-looking, the Parker Fly, nevertheless, has a traditional wood body, but one that is covered by a thin layer of plastic. The fingerboard is made of carbon fiber, and the heavy steel frets are designed to last for years.

Paul Reed Smith Custom (1989)

Paul Reed Smith guitars (or PRSs, as they are often called) are among the few recent models that are already collectibles. Their curly maple tops rival Gibson's best Les Paul models.

ture allowed for a larger cutaway and, therefore, provided easier access to the treble notes. With its one humbucker and two single-coil pickups (Gibson and Fender features combined in one single guitar) and, most importantly, its Floyd-Rose vibrato with a locking system, this type of instrument played a major part in the evolution of guitar playing in this era.

Metropolitan Tanglewood Custom acoustic (1997)

Modeled after a guitar produced by National in the 1960s, the Metropolitan Tanglewood is a wonderful combination of vintage kitsch and modern technology. The goal was to duplicate instruments that were then made of a resin called Resoglas. The Metropolitan retains the shape and distinctive design of its referential model, but it is built of wood, considerably improving the tone.

The Return of Double Courses

Crystal Sound and Sturdy Guitars

The 12-string guitar, developed in the United States, probably has its origins in South American instruments, which are often outfitted with pairs of strings. In fact, the guitar and other related instruments used in that part of the world descended from the double-string ancestors brought by the Spanish conquistadors. Popular in the South at the turn of the century, the 12-string guitar was used by blues musicians such as Blind Willie McTell and Leadbelly, who especially appreciated its high volume. Leadbelly was single-handedly responsible for reviving the 12-string guitar which, at that time, was all but forgotten—only a handful of makers, such as Stella, still offered it in their catalogs. Leadbelly died in 1949, but he was rediscovered in the 1960s, encouraging many builders to try offering 12-string guitars again.

On 12-string guitars, the first two pairs of strings (on the treble side), are generally tuned in unison. The next four pairs are tuned in octaves. The extra tension of these high strings requires a more solidly constructed guitar body, and these instruments generally have extra-strong necks and braces.

Bozo Podunavac is the luthier most noted for 12-string guitars. Originally from Yugoslavia, he left his country in 1959 to settle in Chicago. He built his own instruments starting in 1965, and a Japanese company also produced guitars bearing his name, with his consent. His 12-strings are highly appreciated by acoustic musicians such as Leo Kottke.

The 12-string guitar was successful in its transformation to electricity, with Fender offering one from 1965 to 1969. Several companies also had double-necked guitars in their catalogs, one neck a standard 6-string and the other a 12-string. Gibson produced similar double-necked SGs starting in 1962. But the most celebrated electric 12-string guitar was built by Rickenbacker, whose model had a much smaller neck and peghead than those of its competitors.

This reduced proportion was made possible thanks to an ingenious method of positioning the tuning pegs and thanks to a double reinforcement rod that enabled the correction of any neck movement. In the hands of Roger McGuinn, guitar player for The Byrds, the 12-string electric guitar definitely made its mark.

Guild 212 (1970s)

Guild, like most acoustic builders, capitalized on the folk music revival by launching strong and durable 12-string models.

Martin 12-20 (1972)

The Martin people hesitated a long time before deciding to introduce a 12-string guitar line, and even published a little pamphlet to voice their reluctance. In their opinion, the tension of the strings demanded a top that was too rigid, that is, one that didn't conform to the company's tradition. Nevertheless, under public demand, Martin finally launched their first 12-string in 1964: the D12-20, with a rosewood body.

Fender Electric XII (1965)

Fender launched a 12-string electric guitar in 1965, and its production ceased three years later. The instrument's body is similar to the Jazzmaster's, although the peghead has a very unusual look for a Fender instrument.

Baldwin Double Six (ca. 1965)

In 1965, the Baldwin company, who lost out to CBS in the chance to acquire Fender, bought Burns, a British guitar maker of distinctive models. Note the unusual lawn-green sunburst displayed on this instrument dating from the 1960s.

GLOSSARY

ARCH-TOP
This term describes acoustic guitars whose top is curved, as opposed to being flat. This curvature can be obtained either by carving a thick piece of wood (in this case, a "carved-top") or by molding a thin piece of laminated wood into the required shape.

BRIDGE
A piece of wood placed on the soundboard, whose function is to transmit the vibrations from the strings to the top. On flat-top guitars, the bridge is affixed to the top. The strings themselves are attached to the bridge and transmit their vibrations in a longitudinal pattern. On arch-top guitars, the bridge, shaped like an arch, simply sits on the top. Strings run over the bridge and are attached to a tailpiece at the end of the instrument. Vibrations are, therefore, transmitted vertically.

CUSTOM-COLOR
This term was originally used to describe a factory-made colored finish applied to an instrument on special request from the customer. However, many models from the 1950s and 1960s bear finishes designated "custom," though they were not special-ordered and appeared in the catalog.

CUTAWAY
A section of the guitar body which is "cut away" to give the left hand better access to the upper part or register of the fingerboard. Cutaways come in two basic shapes: Florentine (pointed) or Venetian (rounded).

F-HOLES
F-shaped openings, similar to those of a violin, carved in the top of arch-top and thinline electric guitars.

FINGERBOARD
A piece of ebony or rosewood, with mounted frets, adhered to the surface of the neck; this is where the player stops the strings, using the fingers of his left hand.

FLAT-TOP
This term describes an acoustic guitar with a flat soundboard, as opposed to a guitar with a curved top. (See arch-top.)

FRET
A small metal strip located on the fingerboard. (Originally frets were made of gut and were tied around the guitar neck. Later, other materials such as ebony or ivory were used.) By pressing his finger behind a fret and applying tension to the string, the player transforms this fret into a new nut, changing the length of vibrating string and, therefore, the pitch of the note.

HUMBUCKER
A double-coil pickup, typical of Gibson guitars, as opposed to single-coils, more commonly associated with Fender.

NUT
A piece of bone or plastic (or less commonly, ivory or mother-of-pearl) located on the head of the guitar at the end of the fingerboard. The nut is the point at which the scale-length and the vibrating part of the string ends.

PICK
A piece of plastic (or tortoiseshell, wood, metal, or even stone!) that the guitarist holds between his right-hand thumb and index finger and uses to pluck the strings. This technique limits the polyphonic possibilities of right-hand playing, but allows for rapid single-line playing that would be otherwise very difficult to achieve. The use of a pick is common among jazz, blues, rock, and bluegrass musicians.

PICKGUARD
A plate of plastic, tortoise-shell, or metal placed on (or over) the soundboard and located just under the soundhole. This plate protects the guitar from damage that might be caused by the pick or fingers.

SADDLE
The point on the bridge for supporting the strings.

SIDES (OR RIBS)
The sides of the guitar, of varying depths depending on the model, made of plywood or, on acoustic models, of solid wood (generally maple, mahogany, or rosewood).

SLIDE
A term used to describe a style of playing, in which the musician slides an object over the strings. This object might be a bottleneck, or a metal cylinder that the player wears on one of the fingers of his left hand—generally the ring-finger or the little finger. This technique is commonly used by blues or rock musicians on standard guitars without elevated strings. The "slide" object can also be a solid steel bar, held between several left-hand fingers, and, in this case, the instrument rests on the musician's lap. This technique is favored by Hawaiian musicians (on Hawaiian acoustics, Nationals, and lap-steel electrics), and by country and bluegrass

guitarists (on pedal-steels and dobros).

SOLID-BODY

A guitar with a solid body, built of one or several pieces of solid wood, as opposed to hollow-body guitars, whether acoustic or electric.

SOUNDHOLE

Usually, a round opening in the center of an acoustic guitar that allows sound waves to escape from the soundbox. More generally, this term describes any hole, of any shape—including f-holes—found on the guitar top.

SUNBURST

A specific type of finish found on some acoustic guitars, especially Gibsons, and more commonly on electrics. This finish is basically a gradation of color that usually starts out black or dark brown on the outside edge of the soundboard, and moves toward red and then yellow as it approaches the center.

TOP (OR TABLE OR SOUNDBOARD)

The top surface of the guitar, upon which the bridge is placed. On an acoustic guitar, the top or soundboard plays an essential role: by way of the strings, it vibrates to generate sound waves from the soundbox. On an electric solid-body, the top's acoustic function is considerably limited, and its primary purpose is to simply hold the bridge, tailpiece, pickups, and wiring.

TUNING PEGS (OR TUNERS OR MACHINE HEADS)

Mechanical devices on the peghead to which the guitar strings are attached. Their function is to enable the player to adjust the string tension, and, therefore, their pitch.

VIBRATO

A system of springs and a lever that allows the player to control the pitch of a note. By extension, this term is often applied to the physical lever-arm that activates the system.

INDEX

THE BOOK WAS MADE POSSIBLE THROUGH THE ASSISTANCE OF PRIVATE COLLECTORS, SPECIALIZED STORES AND THE MUSEUM OF THE CITY OF NICE, ALL SOURCES FOR THE MODELS PHOTOGRAPHED IN THIS WORK. THE LIST BELOW PROVIDES THE EXACT NAME OF EACH MODEL, TO WHOM IT BELONGS, AND THE PAGE ON WHICH IT IS FOUND IN THE BOOK.

LARS HENRIKSON
(AX IN HAND)
Gibson Super 400 CES (1965), p. 48;
Gibson L-5 CES (1965), p. 50;
Gibson ES 175D (1961), p. 51;
Gibson Byrdland (1960), p. 53;
Gibson ES-335 TD Blonde (1965),
p. 55;
Epiphone Sheraton (1963), p. 74;
Alhambra Regal Made (ca. 1930),
p. 81;
Rickenbacker Frying Pan (ca. 1955),
p. 84;
Fender Telecaster (1954), p. 92;
Fender Esquire (1954), p. 93;
Fender Esquire Custom (1960) p. 94;
Fender Telecaster (1966), p. 96;
Fender Telecaster Custom Blonde
(1966), p. 96;
Fender Esquire Custom Shop
(1990s), p. 97;
Fender Stratocaster (1955), p. 98;
Fender Stratocaster (1965), p. 101;
Fender Stratocaster (1962), p. 101;
Fender Stratocaster Mary Kaye 62,
Reissue , p. 102;
Fender Eric Clapton Stratocaster
(1991), p. 103;
Gibson Les Paul Gold Top (1954),
p. 113;
Gibson Les Paul Custom Prototype
(1953), p. 113;
Gibson Les Paul TV 3/4 (1954),
p. 115;
Les Paul Junior (ca. 1960), p. 115;
Gibson Les Paul Junior (ca. 1960),
p. 115;
Gibson SG Les Paul (1962), p. 118;
Gibson SG Les Paul (1961), p. 118;
Rickenbacker Combo 400 (ca. 1957),
p. 130;
Fender Electric XII (1965), p. 137.

GARY BURNETTE
(BEE-3 VINTAGE)
Martin 0-45 (1929), p. 32;
Martin D-28 (1933), p. 34;
Martin 00-18 (1932), p. 35;
Martin D-18 (1937), p. 36;
Martin D-28 Sunburst (1937), p. 37;

Martin Jumbo Custom Sunburst
(1985), p. 39;
Gibson Lloyd Loar F-5 (1924), p. 46;
Gibson L-5 CES (1978), p. 50;
Gibson Advanced Jumbo Prototype
(ca. 1935), p. 56;
Gibson L-00 (1937), p. 57;
Gibson J-35 (1939), p. 58;
Gibson J-45 (1953), p. 58;
Gibson Southern Jumbo (1946),
p. 58;
Gibson Montana Custom Advanced
Jumbo (1990s), p. 62;
Gibson Southern Jumbo Montana
(1990s), p. 63;
Fender Stratocaster (1957), p. 99;
Rickenbacker 360-12 (1990s),
p. 131.

COLLECTION OF THE CITY
MUSEUM OF NICE
Antonio de Torres guitar (1884),
p. 18.
François Bastien guitar (1826),
p. 17;
François Breton lyre-guitar (ca.
1800), p. 15;
Gérard Deleplanque guitar, p. 15;
Giovanni Tesler guitar (1618), p. 11;
Jean Christophle guitar, p. 13;
Jean-Joseph Fontanelli bass lute
(1773), p. 10;
lyre-guitare (anonymous, 18th c.),
p. 14;
Pacquet harpguitar (1785), p. 15;
Pierre Pacherel guitar (1834), p. 17;
René Voboam guitar (17th c.), p. 12;

BUCK SULCER
(GUITAR NETWORK)
Fender Telecaster with Bigsby (1969),
p. 97;
Fender Mustang (1970s), p. 105;
Fender Bronco (1967), p. 106;
Fender Coronado II (1967), p. 107;
Gibson Les Paul Silverburst (1981),
p. 119;
Gibson L-6S Deluxe (ca. 1975),
p. 123;
Gretsch Roc Jet (1974), p. 133;

Paul Reed Smith (1989), p. 135;
Baldwin Double Six (ca. 1965),
p. 137.

FRANÇOIS CHARLE
Martin 2-27 (ca. 1870), p. 30; Martin
000 C-16 (1992), p. 39;
Nick Lucas Gibson special (1928),
p. 56;
Gibson Tenor TG-0 (ca. 1930),
p. 57;
Alain Queguiner modèle Jumbo
(1996), p. 67;
Franck Cheval modèle Orville (1995),
p. 67;
Selmer Harp Concert model, p. 72;
Di Mauro modèle Jazz, p. 73;
Weissenborn Style 2 (ca. 1930),
p. 83.

ISABELLE (LA GUITARRERIA)
George Lowden guitar, p. 23;
Hernanos flamenco (1994),
p. 25.
Jeronimo Peña guitar (1978), p. 23;
Kazuo Sato guitar (1995),
p. 23;
Manuel Contreras guitar (1992),
p. 21;
Maurice Dupont flamenco,
p. 24;
Paulino Bernabe guitar, p. 21;

GUY BRUNO
(WOW! NICE GUITARS!)
Gibson B.B. King Lucille (1995),
p. 55;
Oahu Tonemaster (ca. 1930),
p. 85;
National Chicagoan (1948), p. 85;
Fender Lone Star Stratocaster (1997),
p. 103;
Martin 12-20 (1972), p. 136;
Mosrite Fantasy Model, p. 132.

CHRISTIAN SEGURET
Martin 0-18 (1933), p. 34;
Martin 000-18 (1945), p. 35;
Martin D-18 (1944), p. 36;
Martin D-28 (1937), p. 37;

Gibson L-C Century (1935), p. 57;
Fender Telecaster (1957), p. 94.

THIERRY LOYER
Favino (1970s), p. 73;
National Style 1 (1929), p. 78;
R.Q. Jones (ca. 1978), p. 80;
Sheerhorn (1994), p. 80;
Gelas hawaiienne (ca. 1930), p. 82;
Gibson EH-150 (ca. 1937), p. 85.

ANDERSON GUITARS
Fender Lefty Stratocaster (1965),
p. 101;
Fender Princeton amp (1958),
p. 99;
Gibson ES-335 TD (1965), p. 55;
Gibson ES-355 TDSV (1965), p. 55;
Gibson Les Paul Custom (1955),
p. 115.

STEVE PECK
Martin D-45 Custom (1993), p. 38;
Gibson J-100 (1992), p. 59;
Guild T-100 (1961), p. 132;
Martin GT-75 (ca. 1965), p 132.

CHRISTA DAVIS
(WINTER SOUND CO.)
Gibson J-200 (1996), p. 59;
Gibson Nick Lucas Bozeman
(1990s), p. 63;
Fender Stratocaster American
Standard (1993), p. 103;
Steinberger GM 7 (1980s), p.134.

ABALON VINTAGE GUITARS
Taylor Gerry Buckley 614 GB (1995),
p. 67;
Gibson Flying V (1958), p. 120;
Gibson GA 77 amp (1958), p. 120;
Gretsch Streamliner 6190 (1955),
p. 126.

JEFF EVANS
Epiphone Sorrento (1966), p. 75;
Fender Duo-Sonic II (1966), p. 105;
Gibson Firebird III (1968), p. 122;
Gretsch Double Anniversary (1964),
p. 126.

RANDY MULLINS
(GUITARS PLUS)
Gibson Hummingbird (1970s), p. 61;
Gibson Dove (1960 Reissue), p. 61;
Epiphone Triumph (1943), p. 75.

PRIVATE COLLECTION
Benedetto Cremona (1990s), p. 71;
D'Aquisto New Yorker (1987), p. 71;
Guidon (1995), p. 72.

MARTY'S MUSIC
Fender Super Amp (1957), p. 99;
Fender Jazzmaster (1965), p. 105;
Gibson Les Paul Historic Flametop
(1996), p. 120.

RUSSEL "LAWBELLY" MILLS
Gibson Artist model Mandolin
(1906), p. 44;
Gibson L-5 (1937), p. 49.

MIKE AMOS
Gibson Style O Artist (1919), p. 45;
Gibson L-1 (1912), p. 45.
Johnny Milteer (Johnny's Guitar)
Gibson ES 150 (1941), p. 51;
National Duolian (1937), p. 79.

MOTOYOSHI TAKASHIMA
(FIRST GUITAR)
Gibson ES-335 TD (1963), p. 54;
Gibson Les Paul Sunburst (1960),
p. 116.

DARRELL S. YOUNG
(REAL TIME SIGHT AND SOUND)
Gibson J-180 (1992), p. 60;
Washburn (1899), p. 64-65.

ROD HODGENS
(BACK DOOR MUSIC)
Larrivée LC-10 (1990s), p. 66;
Parker Fly Deluxe (1996), p. 135.

CHARLES JOHNSON
Santa Cruz Vintage Artist (1995),
p. 67;
Gretsch Streamliner 6102 (ca. 1970),
p. 127.

FRANÇOIS GUIDON
D'Angelico New Yorker (1963), p. 70;
Fender D'Aquisto (ca. 1975),
p. 71.

BRUCE RICKARD
Gibson ES-335 (1967), p. 55;
Fender Telecaster Deluxe (1974),
p. 96.

FREDDIE WOOTEN
(PALMETTO MUSIC)
Fender Bronco (1967), p. 106;
Rickenbacker 360-12
(1990s), p. 131.

MARK HOOVER
(MARK'S VINTAGE GUITARS)
Rickenbacker Combo 450 (1960),
p. 130;
Rickenbacker 615 (1967), p. 131.

LOUIS STELLA
Guitare René Lacôte (ca. 1830),
p. 17

LYNN MICHAEL
Martin OM-28 (1930), p. 35.

STEVE KILBY
Gibson L-7 (1937), p. 49.

DEREK HAWKINS
Gibson Howard Roberts Custom
(1976), p. 52.

KERRY EAST
(EAST COAST GUITARS)
Gibson Tal Farlow (1996), p. 52.

COLEMAN MUSIC
Gibson J-200 (1952), p. 59.

JAY WOLFE
(WOLFE GUITARS)
Heritage Johnny Smith (1990s),
p. 75.

DANIEL KEIGER
Fender Telecaster Thinline (1968),
p. 96.

MORTY BECKMAN
(WORLWIDE GUITARS)
Fender Musicmaster, p. 104.

JEFF WALKER AND JOHN
MONTGOMERIE
(CAROLINA DISCOUNT MUSIC)
Gretsch 6120 (1996), p. 128.

JACK GAUGHF
(GOLD STAR PAWN)
Gretsch Roc Jet (1974), p. 133.

PITTSBURGH GUITARS
Mark VI Vox (ca. 1965),
p. 133.

BIBLIOGRAPHY

Tony Bacon, *The Ultimate Guitar Book,*
Dorling Kindersley, 1991.

Tony Bacon and Paul Day, *The Fender
Book,* Miller Freeman, 1992.

Tony Bacon and Paul Day, *The Gibson
Les Paul Book,* Miller Freeman, 1993.

Tony Bacon and Paul Day, *The Gretsch
Book,* Miller Freeman, 1996.

Walter Carter, *Gibson: 100 Years of An
American Icon,* General Publishing, 1994.

André Duchossoir, *Gibson Electric, The
Classic Years,* Hal Leonard, 1994.

Tom and Mary Ann Evans, *Guitars: From
the Renaissance to Rock,* Oxford University
Press, 1977.

George Gruhn and Walter Carter,
Gruhn's Guide To Vintage Guitar, GPI
Books Miller Freeman, Inc, 1991.

George Gruhn and Walter Carter, *Electric
Guitars and Basses,* GPI 1994.

Mike Longworth, *Martin Guitars:
A History,* Four Maples Press, 1988.

Richard Smith, *The Complete Story of
Rickenbacker Guitars,* Centerstream
Publishing, 1987.

Tom Wheeler, *American Guitars,* Harper
Collins, 1990.

USEFUL ADDRESSES

Lars Henrikson
Ax in Hand
722 1/2 W. Lincoln
DeKalb, IL. 60115
USA
Tel: 815 758 8898

Gary Burnette
Bee-3 vintage
128 Kingsgate Road
Asheville, NC. 28805
USA
Tel: 704 298 2197
Fax: 704 298 0020

Buck Sulcer
Guitar Network
104 N Market St
Frederick, MD. 21701
USA
Tel: 301 694 3231
Fax: 301 694 5912
E-mail: GuitarNetwork@FWP.Net
Web: www.FWP.Net/GuitarNetwork

La Guitarreria
5, rue d'Édimbourg
75008 Paris
Tel: 01 45 22 54 72

Museum of the City of Nice
65, rue de France, 06000 Nice
Tel: 04 93 88 11 34
Fax: 04 93 82 39 79

Rosyne Charle (luthier)
17, galerie Véro-Dodat
75001 Paris
Tel: 01 42 33 38 93

Patrice Bastien Guitar Express
11, place de la Nation
75012 Paris
Tel: 01 43 72 62 33

Mandolin Brothers, LTD
629 Forrest Avenue
Staten Island, NY. 10310
USA
Tel: 718 981 3226
Fax: 718 816 44 16
Web: www.mandoweb.com

Gruhn Guitars Inc.
400 Broadway
Nashville, TN 37203
USA
Tel: 615 256 2033
Fax: 615 255 2021

ACKNOWLEDGEMENTS

The author wishes to offer special thanks to Rosyne and François Charle (of Lutherie Charle, in Paris), Gary and Bonnie Burnette (of Bee-3 Vintage), Lars Henrickson (of Ax in Hand), and to Susi Gott, all of whom contributed greatly to the creation of this book.

Thanks also to the Museum of the City of Nice, and to Thierry Loyer, Isabelle (of La Guitarreria), Francis Lamy, Laurent Comparin, Thomas Jeanneau, Jean-Marie Vallée, Catherine Champagne (Virgin), Patrice Bastien (Guitar Express), François Guidon, Franck Despagnat, Buck Sulcer, and Olivier Andres.

All photographs are by Matthieu Prier, except for:

p. 20 (D.R.), p. 28 (D.R.), p. 29 (D.R.), p. 42 (D.R.), p. 43 (D.R.), p. 47 (D.R.), p. 53 (D.R.), p. 73 (D.R.), p. 78 (Virgin), p. 79 (Virgin), p. 83 (Virgin), p. 90 (D.R.), p. 91 (D.R.), p. 93 (Virgin), p. 97 (Virgin), p.110 (D.R.), p. 111 (D.R.), p. 117 (Virgin).

This book was created by Copyright for Éditions Solar:
Design: Ute-Charlotte Hettler
Page layout: Jacqueline Leymarie
Editor: Nicolas Jeanneau
English editor: Lisa Davidson